NEW
Gatherings

BRONWEN WILD

Hodder & Stoughton

LONDON SYDNEY AUCKLAND

Acknowledgements

The publishers would like to thank the following for their permission to reproduce copyright material in this book:

Harper Collins for the extract on page 65; *The Washington Post* for the extract on page 6; Sidgwick and Jackson for the extract on page 51; James Clarke & Co for the prayers on pages 32 and 36; Victor Gollancz for the extract on page 69.

Every effort has been made to trace and acknowledge ownership of copyright. The publishers will be glad to make suitable arrangements with any copyright holders whom it has not been possible to contact.

For Graham, Timothy and my family

Also, many thanks to Ros and to all the young people who have contributed and shared in New Gatherings

British Library Cataloguing in Publication Data

Wild, Bronwen
New Gatherings
I. title
377.1

ISBN 0 340 57685 5

First published 1992
© Bronwen Wild

Typeset by Wearset, Boldon, Tyne and Wear.
Printed for the educational publishing division of Hodder & Stoughton Ltd, Mill Road, Dunton Green, Sevenoaks, Kent by Athenaeum Press Ltd, Newcastle upon Tyne.

Contents

Preface

Many schools are striving to make acts of collective worship meaningful and relevant occasions in which all pupils can participate, regardless of their personal beliefs.

This book brings together readings from a wide variety of sources, in particular many written by young people themselves, where they express views and concerns which pupils can understand.

These readings invite response – they challenge young people to consider the values and aspirations of others as well as their own. This book provides opportunities for pupils to share actively in collective worship.

Bron Wild's priority is always the pupil – and this focus is reflected in her selection of "New Gatherings".

Helen Morrison
Education Services Adviser – R.E.
Birmingham,
December 1991

Introduction

The 1988 Education Reform Act uses the term "collective worship" – the word "assembly" is never used in the Act.

Collective worship occurs where pupils of different beliefs and attitudes gather together to share common values and experiences.

I believe that this is a valuable and necessary extension of what goes on in the classroom and the wider school. By focusing on aspects of the curriculum that a school considers to be important, acts of worship can help strengthen a sense of belonging in pupils and staff as well as reflecting the aims and values of the school.

New Gatherings has been devised to meet the needs of groups large and small, as defined in the Act. It offers a unique and refreshing selection of readings suitable for the adolescent audience with an emphasis on a common humanity. Much of the material lends itself naturally to "follow up" work, emphasising the fact that collective worship is not isolated from the real life of the school, or indeed the surrounding community.

The readings offer a wide choice of subject, content and style, giving staff and pupils alike some interesting and unexpected thoughts to consider both during and after the assembled meeting. *New Gatherings* draws readings from many sources including children's own writing, poetry, prose and the literature of various faiths. All the readings have received very positive responses from the young people who have shared in them. The less conventional and sometimes unpredictable content of the writings appeals to the adolescent audience, whether in the traditional large group or in the more intimate classroom situation.

Together with the previously published *Gatherings*, *New Gatherings* will offer a unique resource for the busy teacher faced with organising collective worship. There is a comprehensive index which cross-references linked themes. The prayers are short and in keeping with the readings. They may, however, be omitted or be used as a way of re-emphasising the main theme of the readings.

B.W.

August 1991

Rooks Heath High School

Trust

Reading

"How Can You Trust a 17 Year Old?" by *Judy Mann*

One evening I went out and left my son the 17-year-old in charge of his
brother the eight-year-old and his sister the four-year-old. This, I can
assure you was an act of faith.

Not long before, when I had left him in charge and asked him to leave
the side door open for me, he had done precisely that. I had arrived
home at 1 a.m. on a blustery night, only to discover the door standing
wide open. Fortunately, no intruders had got in (it was too cold a night
for them), but a great deal of chilly air had.

I am a firm believer, however, in giving everyone a second chance. I
also believe in having everyone assume certain household
responsibilities, and I see nothing wrong with having an older sibling
babysit. On this occasion, the task was made somewhat less onerous by
the presence of his girlfriend. I left with complete confidence that the
two would do a wonderful job of babysitting the younger children, and
the younger children would do a wonderful job of chaperoning the
older children.

Later that evening, I discovered that complete confidence was the last
thing I should have left home with.

I had decided to return earlier than planned so that my son and his
girlfriend could go out and have a good time. I called with this happy
news. But instead of hearing his cheerful, grateful voice on the other
end of the line, all I heard was the sound of the telephone ringing.

It was, I should point out, after 10pm, when the two younger children
should have been in bed, and when the two older children should have
been answering the phone.

Obviously, I had been dialling the wrong number. I dialled again.
Carefully. No one answered. I started to panic. "I'll wring his neck," I
said. I decided that they must be outside. Why they'd be outside at 10.30
on a wintry night I had no idea, but it was the only explanation I could
come up with. I waited a few minutes and dialled again. Still no answer.

"I'll kill him," I said. Finally, in desperation, I called his girlfriend's house. After seemingly countless rings, a miracle occurred: his girlfriend answered the phone. "Yes," she said brightly, "he's right here." He came to the phone. I was not my usual calm, rational self. After all, one of the rules of survival for modern parents is that you can't trust modern teenagers. "Where are the children?" I asked. He said they were with him. And he let me know that all my terrible thoughts about what trouble they had got into were quite out of place. They had not gone out joy riding. They had not set the house on fire. They had not overdosed on drugs, alcohol and rock 'n' roll.

They had taken the younger children over to his girlfriend's house to have ice-cream and cake.

This was too wholesome to be believed.

Well, it turned out that I shouldn't have believed it. It was only part of the truth.

On Saturday evening we were at my parents' home commemorating my birthday. I received some lovely gifts and I received some funny gifts – that is, if you happen to think vitamin E, (commonly believed to increase sexual prowess in the aged) and walking canes are funny!

And then my older son gave me the children's gifts.

Mounted and framed were a series of fabulous colour photographs of my children, dressed in their best clothes, and wearing their most wonderful expressions. They are pictures to treasure for a lifetime, all taken by the father of my son's girlfriend. That is what they had really been up to the night they went over to her house for ice-cream and cake.

And that was the most precious gift of all.

Prayer

We do realise that we are not always as trustworthy as we should be. Help us to become worthy of trust and also not to abuse it when given.

Quarrels

Reading

Storms by *Marc Iaccarino (aged 16)*

It seemed that one minute I was fast asleep and then suddenly there was a crash and I leapt up in bed shaking with fright. What was that noise? I sat there for a moment – and then again another crash. It was thunder smashing and crashing in the sky.

I got out of bed, still half asleep and looked out of the window.

It was still dark, but on each crash of thunder the lightning lit up the sky and made the garden come alive. The golden daffodils, which during the day had stood like a troop of soldiers now looked as if a giant had come in the night and flattened them with his great feet.

The wind was roaring like a lion and as it hit the side of the house a long howl was heard just as if some poor animal had been wounded.

The flashes of lightning shot out like long slithers of silver thrown to the ground by some unknown hand.

The trees looked as if they were frantically throwing their branches about like arms trying to protect themselves from the storm.

As suddenly as the thunder started there was silence and then I heard the steady pitter patter of the rain beating against my window.

"Thank goodness", I thought. "The storm is over". But what was that . . . a crash downstairs and raised voices. My parents were still up and arguing again. I could hear my name being mentioned over and over.

I opened my bedroom door and stood on the landing.

My father was saying he didn't want to go but felt he must. My mother was crying and saying over and over again, "I can't go on like this any longer. Why don't you leave?"

I realised there were tears running down my face. I didn't want my parents to split up. Their argument went on and on like the storm, and like the storm it stopped and there was silence.

I crept downstairs and peeped through the gap in the door. My parents were just sitting there and staring at each other.

I stood there unable to move. I wanted to go into the room but my feet wouldn't move. I felt as if I were nailed to the floor. I don't know how long I stood there. I didn't know what to do. I wanted to speak but the words wouldn't come out.

After a while I crept back upstairs and threw myself onto my bed and lay huddled up in a heap holding a cushion against me.

Some time later I heard footsteps coming upstairs and a bedroom door creaked shut and there was silence all around.

Reading

Discord by *Alasdair MacLeod (aged 16)*

High up in my lonely rooftop room
The rafters groan and creak.
Window frames rattle,
The trees sway and moan
In the explosive storm.
Voices downstairs compete
With the howling wind
That beats relentlessly
Against the side of the house.
Inside, the clatter and crash
Of china and ornaments
As they crack and smash against the wall.
The storm outside
Reaches its tumultuous peak.
A distant window fractures and shatters.
While indoors the trade of insults
Becomes an exchange of blows.
As the eye of the storm
Brings an uneasy silence
To the outside world,
The silence inside is equally still.
At long last I fall into
A restless and uncomfortable sleep.

When morning breaks,
The wind outside
Gently coos,
Which is matched inside
By the mournful sobs
Of my unhappy mother.
I shed a sympathetic, involuntary tear
But can say or do nothing.

Prayer

Help us to understand that our loved ones do quarrel and, although we are frightened by this, give us the strength to be there when needed.

Love (1)

Reading

She's My Friend by *Colonel John Mansur*

This story was told as fact and re-written by John Mansur. He heard it in Vietnam but does not know for sure that it is true. As he said, "I do know that stranger things have happened in war."

Whatever their planned target, the mortar rounds landed in an orphanage run by a missionary group in the small Vietnamese village. The missionaries and one or two children were killed outright, and several more children were wounded, including one young girl about eight years old.

People from the village asked for medical help from a neighbouring town that had radio contact with the American forces. Finally, a US doctor and nurse arrived with only their medical kits. They established that the girl was the most critically injured. Without quick action, she would die of shock and loss of blood.

A transfusion was imperative, and a donor with a matching blood type was required. A quick test showed that neither American had the correct type, but several of the uninjured orphans did.

The doctor spoke some pidgin Vietnamese and the nurse a smattering of French. Using that combination, together with much impromptu sign language, they tried to explain to their young, frightened audience that unless they could replace some of the girl's lost blood, she would certainly die. Then they asked if anyone would be willing to give blood to help.

Their request was met with wide-eyed silence. After several long moments, a small hand slowly and waveringly went up, dropped back down, and then went up again.

"Oh, thank you," the nurse said in French. "What is your name?"

"Heng," came the reply.

Heng was quickly laid on a pallet, his arm swabbed with alcohol, and a needle inserted in his vein. Through this ordeal Heng lay stiff and silent.

After a moment, he let out a shuddering sob, quickly covering his face with his free hand.

"Is it hurting, Heng?" the doctor asked. Heng shook his head, but after a few moments another sob escaped, and once more he tried to cover up his crying. Again the doctor asked him if the needle hurt, and again Heng shook his head.

But now his occasional sobs gave way to a steady, silent crying, his eyes screwed tightly shut, his fist in his mouth to stifle his sobs.

The medical team became concerned. Something was obviously very wrong. At this point, a Vietnamese nurse arrived to help. Seeing the little one's distress, she spoke to him rapidly in Vietnamese, listened to his reply and answered him in a soothing voice.

After a moment, the patient stopped crying and looked questioningly at the Vietnamese nurse. When she nodded, a look of great relief spread over his face.

Glancing up, the nurse said quietly to the Americans, "He thought he was dying. He misunderstood you. He thought you had asked him to give all his blood so the little girl could live."

"But why would he be willing to do that?" asked the Navy nurse.

The Vietnamese nurse repeated the question to the little boy, who answered simply, "She's my friend."

Greater love has no man than this, that he lay down his life for his friends.

Prayer

There is little to add to this story of real bravery and love. Today, if we see someone in trouble, give us the courage to help instead of walking by.

Courage

Reading

Sing for Me by *Arthur Milward*

As well as my son, Adrian, there were seven children in his ward at the Great Ormond Street Hospital for Sick Children in London. They ranged from Adrian's four years, through Carolyn, Elizabeth, Joseph, Sammy, Mary and Sally, to twelve year old Freddie.

All the young patients were victims of leukaemia, which in those days meant they didn't have long to live. All, that is, except one – beautiful, green-eyed, golden-haired Elizabeth, who was ten years old. After completing a common regime of therapy with the other children, she would go home and live a healthy life. Yet the other children felt a genuine and profound sympathy for the little girl.

Elizabeth, who had undergone complicated surgery in the region behind her ears, was going deaf. The process was quite advanced, and it would be only a matter of months before her hearing loss was complete – and irreversible. That Elizabeth was an ardent music lover, who possessed a clear and delightful singing voice and showed promise as a pianist, made the prospect of her inevitable deafness all the more tragic. But she never complained. Occasionally, though, when she thought no one was looking, silent tears would form in her eyes and roll down her cheeks.

Elizabeth loved music more than anything else, and she enjoyed listening just as much as she enjoyed performing. Frequently, after I had helped my son prepare for bed, she would beckon me into the playroom, which was quiet after the day's activities. Seating herself in a big leather armchair, and making room for me to sit beside her, she would take my hand and say, "Sing for me."

Certainly no great singer, but capable of carrying a tune, I could not deny her request. Facing her so she could see my lips, and pronouncing as clearly as I could, I would sing a couple of songs for these special "command performances." She would listen intently and with obvious enjoyment, then thank me gravely with a quick kiss.

The other children, as I have said, were disturbed by the little girl's plight and decided to do something to cheer her up. Under Freddie's leadership they came to a decision, which they took to staff nurse Jean Brown.

"Brownie," as she was known to parents and children alike, was a tall, angular young woman, whose formidable manner had been known to strike terror in the casual observer. The children, however, were not deceived by her brusque efficiency. They knew Brownie was their friend.

Initially, Brownie was taken aback by their announcement. "You want to give a concert for Elizabeth's eleventh birthday?" she exclaimed. "And it's in three weeks' time? You're mad." Seeing their crestfallen faces, she added, "You're all mad. But I'll help you."

Brownie lost no time in keeping her promise. She hurried to the telephone in the nurses' sitting-room and dialled the number of a conservatory of music, not a great distance away in North London. "Kindly give a message to Sister Mary Joseph," she instructed the receptionist. "Tell her to expect a visit this evening from Jean Brown on important business."

As soon as she was off duty, Brownie took a taxi to the conservatory to see her friend, Sister Mary Joseph, who was a voice and choir teacher. After a brief greeting, the nun came right to the point. "Brownie," she asked, "what hare-brained scheme do you intend to involve me in now?"

"Mary J," replied Brownie, "is it possible to transform a small group of children, none of whom has had any musical training, into a passable choir, capable of giving a concert in three weeks' time?"

"It is possible," replied Sister Mary Joseph. "Not very probable, but possible."

"Bless you, Mary J," exclaimed the nurse. "I knew you would."

"Just a minute, Brownie," said the nun. "Tell me more. Maybe I am unworthy of your blessing."

Twenty minutes later, the two parted on the steps of the conservatory. "Bless you, Mary J," repeated Brownie. "We'll see you on Wednesday at three."

"Called what?" demanded Freddie incredulously as Brownie confronted him and the other children while Elizabeth was undergoing her daily therapy. "Is she a man or a woman, then? How can she be called 'Mary Joseph'?"

"She's a nun, Freddie. She teaches at one of the best music schools in

London. It'd cost you two guineas an hour to take lessons from her. And she's going to train you – for free."

"Blimey!" interjected Sammy who knew the value of a shilling because his mother kept a stall in London's Sunday-morning market in Petticoat Lane. Brushing aside Freddie's objections, Sammy said, "We'll take it."

So it was settled. Under Sister Mary Joseph's able direction, the children practised each day while Elizabeth was undergoing therapy. There was only one major problem: how to include nine-year-old Joseph in the concert. Clearly, Joseph could not be left out, but he could no longer use his vocal cords.

"Joseph," the nun told him, after she had noticed him watching wistfully as the others were assigned their singing parts, "I believe Our Lord wants you to help me in a very special way at the concert. You have the same name as I have, and He wants you to work quite closely with me. You will sit beside me and turn the music pages as I play."

For a brief moment, Joseph's eyes shone. Then, close to tears, he scribbled frantically on his note pad. "But Sister, I can't read music."

Sister Mary Joseph smiled down at the anxious little boy. "Don't worry," she assured him, "you will. Our Lord and I will work on it."

Incredibly, within the three-week deadline, the Lord, Sister Mary Joseph and Brownie transformed six dying children, none of whom had any noticeable musical talent, into an acceptable choir, and a little boy who could neither sing nor speak into a confident page-turner.

Equally remarkable, the secret was well kept. Elizabeth's surprise as she was led into the hospital chapel on the afternoon of her birthday and seated on a "throne" (a wheelchair) was genuine. Her pretty face flushed with excitement, and she leaned forward to listen.

Although the audience – ten parents and three nurses – sat only a few feet from the platform, we had some difficulty in seeing the faces of the choristers clearly. But we didn't have any trouble hearing them as they worked through a somewhat incongruous repertoire that ranged from *Jesus Loves Me* to *Danny Boy* – all favourites of Elizabeth's. "Remember to sing *loud*," Sister Mary Joseph had admonished the choristers just before the programme began. "You know she can hear very little, so give it all you've got." And they did.

The concert was a great success. Elizabeth said it was the best birthday she had ever had. The choir almost burst with pride. Joseph beamed. The rest of us, I'm afraid, shed more tears.

I have no printed programme to show for the most memorable of all the concerts I have attended. No rave reviews were written.

Nevertheless, I have never heard, nor do I expect to hear, more beautiful music. If I close my eyes, I can still hear every note.

Those six young voices have been stilled now these many years. All seven members of the choir – the six choristers and the silent page-turner – are sleeping. But I guarantee that Elizabeth, now married and the mother of her own golden-haired, green-eyed daughter, can still hear, in the ear of her memory, those six voices which were among the last sounds she ever heard.

Prayer

Thank you for the gift of hearing. We ask your blessing on all those who are deaf.

Breaking down the walls

Reading

So This is Christmas by *Rabia Rasheed (aged 16)*
(Inspired by the events in November 1989)

The fatigued nurse loosened her shoes and slipped into the chair. She selected a magazine from the table and began to read it in the subdued light of the hospital room. In front of her, on the bed, lay a plump elderly man connected to a heart machine and various other implements. The blonde haired nurse had soon become accustomed to the regular bleeping of the heart machine and she yawned, almost falling asleep. Suddenly the bleep of the machine slowed and it was the change in its rhythm which aroused her. She rose immediately, checked the machine and called for the doctor. She stood there waiting but did not know that the patient, Dieter, could feel his soul slowly drifting. Something, though, which had long been buried within him now anchored it. This tiny mass of dreams which he knew was impossible now battled with the reality and took over his soul and mind. It aroused the dead soldier who had once fought for freedom and it now fought for this hope, this absurd dream, this life and it brought him back to consciousness.

As Dieter opened his eyes the blurred vision soon became clear. The bearded doctor was leaning over him and the fresh faced nurse stood at the corner of the bed holding some things. Dieter could hear the doctor saying, in German, "It's all right," and he managed a muffled reply in his native language.

Dieter, a man in his sixties was one of the few Germans who had disagreed with Hitler during World War 2 and had helped the Jews. He was a stout man and his ageing was visible by the partially balding and white hair, the heavy grooves on his forehead and the sagging skin under his eyes. He was ashamed of his native background. Now he had no reward for his good deeds, he had lost his business and had been separated from his family.

Two weeks had passed and Dieter had recovered considerably. He sat in the common room watching the television for a reason he did not know because all that was broadcast in East Germany was what the government thought "suitable" for people to see. He hated the hypocrisy – the way everything was made to seem wonderful when in reality it was quite the opposite. Because of his illness and the fact that he lived in some isolation in the countryside, Dieter had not been following the changes in his country.

Surprisingly, for the first time, the news did not follow the normal format and there was a reporter "live" from a demonstration and Dieter actually watched. It explained that the demonstrators were Catholics commemorating those who had died during the War. He sat there, his eyes filling with tears. It all brought back memories, sad memories. As soon as he let his eyelids drop he could picture vivid images of the loved ones he had lost . . . he was the only one to survive.

When he reopened his eyes, the television showed how to get passports and papers to cross the Berlin Wall. Dieter's jaw dropped as he sat wide-eyed in disbelief. His heart pumped faster but he managed to calm himself. He wanted to be sure that this was true – he did not want to raise his hopes for nothing. Soon he saw images of people standing on the wall, people travelling in cars from East to West, people embracing each other. Yes, at last his dream was coming true! There was a tingling inside him – there was a dream in his eyes that had once disappeared and there was a surge of hope in his heart which was once forgotten.

He *had* to become well now, to be able to join the celebrations at Christmas. Christmas, for Dieter, had lost its meaning since he had been separated from his family.

Dieter, fully recovered, sat leaning against the back of the seat, gazing out of the window of the train taking him back to his farm. He calculated that there were three more days left before Christmas. The train eventually stopped at his station and he exited hastily, carrying his battered suitcase. Turning left from the station he continued his journey through the narrow, winding lanes of the countryside towards his farm.

He opened the wooden gate with his large rough hands and he looked around. The farm was not very large with only a barn and a simple house in the centre, surrounded by fields. He entered his house and noticed that the dust had piled on the shelves. He unscrewed the sugar jar and counted his savings. Luckily there was enough money, which he placed in his wallet.

Next day he took the train to Berlin and arrived in the evening. Berlin was very crowded and there was excitement in the faces of everyone. He collected the necessary papers from the office in the square and it was here that he met Hans for the first time. Hans, slightly younger than Dieter, had also experienced the War and together they remembered the past and showed each other photographs of their families. During their conversation Hans discovered that Dieter had nowhere to stay on Christmas Eve and cordially invited him to his cousin's house.

Christmas Day and Dieter was awake early and enjoyed his traditional German breakfast prepared for him by Hans's cousin. He was most grateful for their generosity and spent the day with Hans and his cousin's family, participating in the festive activities. The day passed quickly as Dieter was enjoying himself.

That evening Dieter sat in his room, with the old tan suitcase open. He pulled from it his smartest suit. As he admired himself in the mirror he noticed how old he had grown and how much time had passed, but *inside* he felt young and vigorous. Together with Hans he made his way to the Wall. The streets were a friendly jungle of people and the two elderly men weaved their way through. The crowd was immense near the Wall, but the younger generation seemed to have a respect for the old and allowed them to pass through.

It was a chilly night but Dieter felt the warmth and enthusiasm amidst the people. There was much noise, shouting and laughter in the crowd. Dieter joined hands with those on either side of him and began to sing a well known German hymn. Others who heard joined in and more and more people joined until the crowd's shouting became a murmur and eventually the whole crowd was chanting. People from the West who had been sitting on the Wall jumped down, linked hands and began to sing. The sound rose to a great height and resonated through every part of Dieter's body. This, thought Dieter, was the sound of Unity! As the song ended people cheered. A man from the West, who Dieter did not even know, embraced him. The embrace was an ecstatic flow of affection and sincerity which brought tears to Dieter's eyes. Suddenly, an array of fireworks was set off which whizzed, popped and exploded, illuminating the sky with bright colours. Dieter stood, entranced and then applauded with the crowd. Seeing the tremendous liveliness Dieter knew he had lived only to see this awakening. He thought about how people built walls between them and only they could break them down.

He knew that differences had been overcome in a most miraculous way. He thought, "This is rejoicing! This is Christmas!"

Prayer

If walls have been built, help us be the ones to break them down. May we have an open mind and a sympathetic outlook to difficulties we come across.

Aspects of childhood

Reading

Two Poems by *Alasdair MacLeod (aged 16)*

The Baby

In the early morning,
From the peace and quiet
A Piercing cry
Comes from the room next door.
"The baby's awake," says a tired voice.
"It's your turn,"
But all that can be heard
From the sleeping husband
Is a quiet snoring,
And so the tired wife
Crawls wearily out of bed
And stumbles in
To comfort her troubled child.
She picks him up,
And takes him downstairs,
To get his bottle
Of warm milk.

She lays him in
His pram by the window, and opens the curtains
To let in
An early morning scene.
The sun has not yet risen,
But the silent street is palely lit
By the street lamps and the pre-dawn glow.
The baby begins
To look about,
Watching the trees
Blow gently in the wind.
The movement of the leaves
Fascinates the child.
He raises his hand,
As if to touch
The moving leaves.
Then he takes
The toy in his pram
And grips it firmly
As if his tiny life depended on it.
In an instant the little hands
Become disinterested
In the toy,
And release their grip.
Then the wife
Returns with a bottle
Of warm milk.
The baby begins to suck
The warm milk
From the bottle.
In a few minutes
It's all gone,
And his little face
Reflects sheer contentment.
He is returned to his cot
By his tired mother,
Who returns to bed.
The little child
Is still grinning
As he drifts off into a satisfied sleep.

Everything and Nothing

The sad and lonely boy crouched in the corner
Of his warm, cosy room.
A clock on the wall whirred and clicked,
Its hands glowing green in the dark,
Ticking away the long, dark hours of the night.
His large bed stood in the corner of the room,
Puffed high with its heavy quilt.
The huge toy cupboard doors, half closed,
Filled the wall by the door.
Toys were crammed onto all the shelves.
A train set ran all around the room,
The model trains parked in their sheds.
A cassette recorder rested on the shelf above the bed,
Tapes and books neatly stacked beside it,
All gathering dust,
All unused for days.
All unwanted gifts,
For a lonely little boy,
Who longed for just a little
Love and attention.
But all he got
Were toys and games,
And a visit from his father
Once each week –
When he remembered.

Prayer

In a moment of silence, let us think of children throughout
the world.

Religions (1)

Reading

Are We so Different?

As we go about our daily activities we are aware that there are many different religions and different ideas about God. There are a variety of religions represented in this meeting today, but there are many beliefs held in common, perhaps more than we realise. Let me try to explain what I mean. . . .

In Korea there is a legend about a native warrior who died and went to heaven. "Before I enter," he said to the gate-keeper, "I would like you to take me on a tour of hell." The gate-keeper found a guide to take the warrior to hell. When he got there he was astonished to see a great table piled high with the choicest foods. But the people in hell were starving. The warrior turned to his guide and raised his eyebrows.

"It's this way," the guide explained. "Everybody who comes here is given a pair of chopsticks 2 metres long, and is required to hold them at the end to eat. But you just can't eat with chopsticks that long if you hold them at the end. Look at them. They miss their mouths every time, see?"

The visitor agreed that this was hell indeed and asked to be taken back to heaven post-haste. In heaven, to his surprise, he saw a similar room, with a similar table laden with very choice foods. But the people were very happy; they looked radiantly happy.

The visitor turned to the guide. "No chopsticks, I suppose?" he said.

"Oh yes," said the guide, "they have the same chopsticks, the same length and they must be held at the end, just as in hell. But you see, these people have learned that if a man feeds his neighbour, his neighbour will feed him also."

That story comes from Korea, so it is possible that the writer could have been a Buddhist. If you think of the meaning of the story it is "helping others". This is one of the basic teachings of many of the world's great religions.

Another time we shall look at some of these teachings in more detail and try to see for ourselves just how similar the religions are.

Prayer

Let us conclude today with the words of an African proverb
– "Three things are important in this world: Good health,
Peace with one's neighbour, Friendship with all . . ."
by Seker

Religions (2)

Reading

Are We so Different?

On a previous occasion, we discovered one of the basic teachings of many of the world's great religions. In fact, all groups of people, religious and non-religious, will probably agree on one important principle for the good of the human race, "Do to others what you would have them do to you." Yet, so often we dwell on how *different* people are. We dismiss suspiciously things we do not understand and we are inclined to reject someone who is different in some obvious way – colour, creed, class, race or sex. I'd like to ask you a question . . . "Are we really so very different?"

In the case of religion, despite the differences there *are* many similarities. For example, most religions have:

> a God
> a founder
> a holy book
> a place of worship
> a place of pilgrimage
> prayer
> festivals
> initiation rites (for birth, marriage and death)

Nearly all religions demand a great deal from their members. They must attend services and join together to worship, and members must live according to the rules of their religion. All religions give a set of values which make the world a better place for people to live in. All religions say that murder, theft and selfishness are evil and that people should treat others as they themselves would wish to be treated.

The Hindu religion has developed in India over a period of 6,000 years. Hindus worship many gods and goddesses, but these represent different aspects of the one God. Buddhism is also from India, but Buddhists do not speak of "God" at all. Judaism is the religion of the

Jews, practised by them in many countries for over 4,000 years. Their strong belief in the One God has passed into Christianity and Islam. These three religions originated in the Middle East. The Sikh religion is the youngest of the major world religions, founded 500 years ago in India. Sikhs believe in the One God, and in freedom and equality for all.

One of the world's largest religions is Buddhism. The Buddha means "Enlightened One" and Gautama, the founder, is said to have received full enlightenment about the mystery of life and suffering, and taught it to his followers. So, they go to him for help and try to follow his example.

Buddhist writings from Samyutta Nikaya say:

> No altar-fires for me, no word for sacrifices,
> The fire I light is right inside myself,
> Burning bright and warm.
> My life is my sacrifice,
> My heart is the altar,
> For I am a disciple of the Buddha,
> The fire is my own true self, my servant.

Here are six important things from the sayings of Muhammad:

> Speak the truth.
> Carry out your promises.
> Keep true to your responsibilities
> Be pure in thought and action.
> Keep your hands from violence,
> And from taking anything unlawful and bad.

Jesus said:

> A new commandment I give you: love one another.
> As I have loved you, so you must love one another.
> If you have love for one another,
> then all will know that you are my disciples.

Here is a Sikh prayer by Guru Gobind:

> God, grant me this prayer:
> May I never turn away from the chance of doing good,
> May I never be afraid when I have to fight adversity,
> May I never lose control when I win a victory,

I want, always, to have control over my heart:
This is what I want most from your goodness.

This is a Jewish prayer:

May the Lord bless you and keep you,
May the Lord make His face to shine upon you
And be gracious unto you
Now, and forever. Amen

For some people, a religion does not offer fulfilment. Humanists argue that there is a meaning to life without God and if human problems are to be solved at all they will only be solved by human beings.

Humanists value people and their happiness. They value our human powers of reasoning and imagining and they value love. These qualities are fundamental because they make us distinctively human. Although Humanists do not believe in a God-given code of behaviour they do have a great regard for sincerity, fairness and compassion. They try to behave responsibly and thoughtfully, rejecting the temptation to exploit or cheat anyone.

Even though we may not worship in the same way, we can learn to respect the beliefs of other people by some understanding of their ideas. It is only by understanding and respect that we can live happily together.

. So, I ask you the question, "Are we so very different?" Are we not taking various roads to the same goal? Think about it.

Prayer

Let us accept the fact that all of us are different.
May we be tolerant and have understanding of people who see God in different ways.
Teach us how we can learn to live in unity regardless of differences.

Alone

Reading

Dumb Insolence by *Adrian Mitchell*

I'm big for ten years old
Maybe that's why they get at me

Teachers, parents, cops
Always getting at me

When they get at me

I don't hit em
They can do you for that

I don't swear at em
They can do you for that

I stick my hands in my pockets
And stare at them

And while I stare at them
I think about sick

They call it dumb insolence

They don't like it
But they can't do you for it

I've been done before
They say if I get done again

They'll put me in a home
So I do dumb insolence

Reading

Dumb Insolence by *Robert Meadows (aged 16)*
(Inspired by the poem of the same title.)

I look back on my life and I wish I had listened to the people who knew.
They told me what would happen, but I would never listen or believe
them. Big me – I always knew best. Now look where I am. People tried
to help me. There were threats and warnings from the police. You
know, when I was younger, I used to do something to stop me laughing
at people. I would think of SICK, yes, sick! Then, I'd stick my hands
into my pockets and stare straight into their eyes. I don't know how it
used to help, but looking back on it I know it did. I know it always used
to stop me swearing or hitting them – that would have got me into more
trouble.

You know, believe it or not, I hated being in trouble, but really that's
all I ever used to do. It all went wrong, you see. The real reason I did
those things was probably because when I was younger I did not have
many friends. Nobody seemed to like or care for someone like me. I was
a sad boy, my childhood was nothing. There was no-one to play with,
nobody to talk to – I was a lonely child. Somehow Mum and Dad were
always too busy for me. According to them I was just a nuisance,
something else for them to tend to. I just wanted someone to give me a
bit of attention, someone to show they cared, someone to talk to,
someone who would, could, give me some time in the day. I needed
someone who understood the way I felt, who would help me when I
needed someone.

You know that really, deep inside, I felt sick – sick of stealing, sick of
pretending. I just wanted people to accept me for what I was. Why did I
have to do these things? Nobody else did, so why was I different? It was
unfair! My life was ruined because people would not accept me for what
I was. That was all I ever wanted – people to like me, to be my friends.
Was that too much to ask; for someone to trust and to be my friend?

I tried not to care; I thought *that* in itself would take me through life,
but look how I have ended up in this place. I never thought I would miss
my Mum and Dad, but I do, you know. They were right – I did end up
in a home. I often blamed my parents, thinking that if they had spent
more time caring for me I would never have ended up here. I
sometimes wished that I had been born where people might have cared
for me.

My life is finished. I just want to get out of here but there's nowhere to go. The cops never liked me. They're probably glad I'm shut up in here. They've got rid of me. I think that if I had had more friends and people who cared for me I would never have got into trouble and then I would not have started using (as I call it) "dumb insolence". I must admit that it worked well for a time anyway.

But, it's led me here, so now I have to live with it.

Prayer

Help me to listen to criticism of myself, to accept the truth and so to learn. Give me the courage to say "I'm sorry" and to understand that loving doesn't always mean that I should get my own way.

Time

Reading

When Did You Last Think About Time?

If you had a bank that credited your account each morning with £86,400, that carried over no balance from day to day – allowed you to keep no cash in your account – and every evening cancelled whatever part of the amount you had failed to use during the day, what would you do? Draw out every penny every day, of course, and use it to your advantage!

Well, you have such a bank – and its name is TIME. Every morning it credits you with 86,400 seconds. Every night, it rules off as lost whatever of this you have failed to invest to good purpose. It carries over no balances. It allows no overdrafts. If you fail to use the day's deposits, the loss is yours. There is no going back. There is no drawing against "tomorrow." It is up to each of us to invest the precious fund of hours, minutes and seconds in order to get from it the utmost in health, happiness and success.

When did you last think of TIME? When you were late for something or when you had something to look forward to? Do these sayings sound familiar to you?

"I didn't have time to get the project done . . ."

"What time do you call this?"

"Sorry I'm late – I overslept . . ."

"Time flies."

"You can *make* time to do it!"

Time is something we hardly ever think deeply about, but it has become one of the main influences in our lives.

For some people time passes very quickly whilst for others it seems to go extremely slowly. When you can't do an exam, an hour can be an eternity ticking by. Think of that same hour at lunchtime – how quickly it goes! I am sure you can think of examples you have experienced yourself.

You might think that a day is quite a long time, but when you consider a day in relation to the thousands and millions of years that have gone by in the past, it is a very short time indeed.

You might think of Christ's birth as part of ancient history – but it was only 620 thousand days ago. The Norman invasion of England was only 331 thousand days ago. And if you are fourteen years old you have been around for a mere five thousand one hundred and 40 days!

We must also remember that time stretches forward into the future. No one knows just how far, and so we use the term "infinity", meaning for ever.

It is very difficult to get away from time and it is related to your personal life very closely. As one controversial comedian described . . . "We spend our lives on the run. We get up by the clock, go to work by the clock, eat and sleep by the clock, get up again, go to work – and then we retire. And what do they give us? A CLOCK. . . !"

You probably have a usual getting-up time, a leaving-for-school time, a lunch time and a tea time. In these cases time is being used as a practical way of making sure you are where you need to be, and that you don't miss things.

School starts at a regular time and because the time is the same for all pupils, they arrive together and start lessons at the same time (or should do!)

Buses and trains run to a timetable so that people can predict when to leave and when they will arrive at their destination. Football matches start at a stated time – again so that spectators know when to get to the ground.

At the beginning, I said that it was up to you to use the precious fund of time to get the most from it.

Prayer

I don't want to waste the minutes and hours
That have been given to me.
Help me to work out
The things I have to do today.
There are probably only
One or two important things.
Give me the courage
To tackle those things first
And then show me
That I do have the time
To listen,
Time for kindness,
Time for laughter,
Time for love.
Help me not to be
Too busy to live.
  by Frank Topping

Love (2)

Reading

A Sandpiper to bring you joy by *Mary Sherman Hilbert*

Several years ago, a neighbour related an experience she had on the beach one winter. The incident so haunted me that later I set down what she had said.

She was six years old when I first met her on the beach near where I live. I drive to this bit of the coast, a distance of three or four miles, whenever the world begins to close in on me.

She was building a sand-castle or something and looked up, her eyes as blue as the sea.

"Hallo," she said. I answered with a nod, not really in the mood to bother with a small child.

"I'm building," she said.

"So I see. What is it?" I asked, not caring.

"Oh, I don't know. I just like the feel of the sand."

That sounds good, I thought, and slipped off my shoes. A sandpiper glided by.

"That's a joy," the child said.

"It's what?"

"It's a joy. My mummy says sandpipers come to bring us joy."

The bird went glissading down the beach. "Goodbye, joy," I muttered to myself, "hallo, pain," and turned to walk on. I was depressed; my life seemed completely out of balance.

"What's your name?" She wouldn't give up.

"Ruth," I answered. "I'm Ruth Peterson."

"Mine's Windy." It sounded like Windy. "And I'm six."

"Hallo, Windy."

She giggled. "You're funny," she said. In spite of my gloom I laughed too and walked on.

Her musical giggles followed me. "Come again, Mrs P," she called. "We'll have another happy day."

The days and the weeks that followed belonged to someone else: a group of unruly Scouts, school meetings, an ailing mother.

The sun was shining one morning as I finished washing up. "I need a sandpiper," I said to myself, gathering up my coat.

The never-changing balm of the sea-shore awaited me. The breeze was chilly, but I strode along, trying to recapture the serenity I needed. I had forgotten the child and was startled when she appeared.

"Hallo, Mrs P," she said. "Do you want to play?"

"What did you have in mind?" I asked, with a twinge of annoyance.

"I don't know. *You* say."

"How about charades?" I asked sarcastically.

The tinkling laughter burst forth again. "I don't know what that is."

"Then let's just walk." Looking at her, I noticed the delicate fairness of her face.

"Where do you live?" I asked.

"Over there." She pointed towards a row of holiday chalets. *Strange*, I thought, *in winter*.

"Where do you got to school?"

"I don't go to school. Mummy says we're on holiday."

She chattered little-girl talk as we strolled along the beach, but my mind was on other things. When I left for home, Windy said it had been a happy day. Feeling surprisingly better, I smiled at her and agreed.

Three weeks later, I rushed to my beach in a state of near panic. I was in no mood even to greet Windy. I thought I saw her mother in their doorway and felt like demanding that she keep her child at home.

"Look, if you don't mind," I said crossly when Windy caught up with me, "I'd rather be alone today." She seemed unusually pale and out of breath.

"Why?" she asked.

I turned on her and shouted, "Because my mother's died!" – and thought, *My God, why am I saying this to a little child?*

"Oh," she said quietly, "then this is a bad day."

"Yes, and yesterday and the day before that and – oh, go away!"

"Did it hurt?"

"Did *what* hurt?" I was exasperated with her, with myself.

"When she died?"

"Of *course* it hurt!" I snapped, misunderstanding, wrapped up in myself. I strode off.

A month or so after that, when I next went to the beach, she wasn't there. Feeling guilty, ashamed, and admitting to myself I missed her, I went up to the chalet after my walk and knocked at the door. A drawn looking young woman with honey coloured hair opened the door.

"Hallo," I said. "I'm Ruth Peterson. I missed your little girl today and wondered where she was."

"Oh, yes, Mrs Peterson, please come in. Wendy talked of you so much. I'm afraid I allowed her to bother you. If she was a nuisance, please accept my apologies."

"Not at all – she's a delightful child," I said, suddenly realising that I meant it. "Where is she?"

"Wendy died last week, Mrs Peterson. She had leukaemia. Maybe she didn't tell you."

Struck dumb, I groped for a chair. My breath caught.

"She loved this place; so when she asked to come, we couldn't say no. She seemed so much better here and had a lot of what she called happy days. But the last few weeks she declined rapidly. . . ." Her voice faltered. "She left something for you . . . if only I can find it. Could you wait a moment while I look?"

I nodded stupidly, my mind racing for something, anything, to say to her.

She handed me a smeared envelope, with MRS P printed in bold, childish letters.

Inside was a drawing in bright crayon colours – a yellow beach, a blue sea, a brown bird. Underneath was carefully printed:

A SANDPIPER
TO BRING YOU JOY

Tears welled up in my eyes, and a heart that had almost forgotten how to love opened wide. I took Wendy's mother in my arms. "I'm sorry, I'm so sorry," I kept repeating, and we wept together.

The precious little picture is framed now and hangs in my study. Six words – one for each year of her life – that speak to me of inner harmony, courage, undemanding love. A gift from a child with sea-blue eyes and hair the colour of sand – who taught me the gift of love.

Prayer

Help me to see good that can be done
The caring that can be offered
The love that can be given.
Whilst I mope about myself
There are people waiting for the kindness I can give.
Help me to give, to share,
To start again a renewed life.
   by Frank Topping

Bully
(The Mind of the Bully)

Reading

The Victim: Richard. The Bully: Does it matter?
by *Louise Hudson (aged 16)*

Outside the sun shines lovingly at the world, but she doesn't shine on me. And inside the compact space of my mind, dark storm clouds gather and rain into my heart.

Along the pavement outside my bedroom window walks Richard and around him glows love. Each strand of his hair is perfect and his clothes are sparkling clean and pressed. Each foot carries a polished shoe; they catch the light and reflect it into my face, blinding me.

On his shoulder a heavy bag, full of neatly ticked exercise books, hangs lightly. And between his ears a treasure chest packed with answers and theories.

As Richard disappears from view, I look around myself at my bedroom as it is called. My life feels a turmoil of reality and deceit. The clothes strewn untidily about, state the reality. The unsuccessful disguise of Dad's after-shave on last week's sweatshirt is the deceit.

The scratched face of my watch tells me to hurry, as I force a comb through my hair. The gel I stole from Woolworth's is finished, so I have to use spit instead.

At school, my brain stretches in an attempt to learn and be intelligent but to no avail. In front of me Richard quietly and modestly impresses the teacher with his position in the maths text book.

When I need help the teacher tries to encourage me towards some modest goal which I know Richard passed long ago.

Inside my head a heat is burning and I feel a deep hatred for Richard whose very presence in the room repulses me. I long to disconnect his intelligence so I can watch and see him fade away.

Tearing a page from the beginning of my exercise book, I start to loop a piece of paper around an elastic band and use Richard's self-assured back for target practice. At first he doesn't notice, but behind and to the side of me my friends are laughing. They don't like Richard either. In fact, I suspect, Richard has no friends at all.

Eventually Richard notices and calmly turns around and asks, "Do you have to be so childish? Shouldn't you be trying to catch up?"

As fire is to paper, my temper ignites. Just then the bell rings and the normal rush to leave the room occurs. I join in the crowd thoughtlessly leaving my work scattered on the desk, while Richard calmly puts his books away.

Everyone around me is completely oblivious to the millions of painful thoughts racing round my mind. I hate Richard. He thinks he is so superior just because he was born with more intellect than I'll ever achieve. So what that he is smartly dressed and scrubbed clean? He has no friends, but I do. I hate Richard. His smart appearance doesn't impress me nor do his high grades. They don't impress anyone except teachers and other people whom I despise just as much.

But deep down hidden behind the ignorant lies that I use to hide myself, I know that Richard does impress me. I would love to want to give myself the time to preen myself every morning to perfection. I would love to be able to work hours and hours without giving up.

So what that Richard has no friends? I have no friends as such, only a group of idiots who hate me but who are too scared to tell me. Nobody needs them except me as I have nothing else. Richard does; he has his family and most of all himself.

So when the classroom door opens and Richard walks out, I punch him and I kick him and I hit his head so hard against the wall that his blood drips down onto his bag. And then I drop him and I ransack his bag, ripping his books to shreds and breaking his pens.

Richard doesn't say anything as I walk away. . . .

Prayer

Let us think for a while in silence about the story we have heard. Can we see anything of ourselves in these two people? Help us to be honest in our response to others. If we know of someone's life being made miserable because of bullying let us have the courage to tell, so that both people can be helped.*

---

*See footnote on page 41

Bully
(Thoughts of the Victim)

Reading

Eddy Jones and Me by *Andrea Spain (aged 16)*

Hello, I'm Eddy Jones's plaything. You don't have to talk to me if you don't want to – I'll understand. You're staying? That's more than anyone else will do. They know I'm his private toy and won't come near me – they're too scared – but who would want to talk to me anyway? Aren't you scared?

Eddy picks on me to show off, but why me? He could pick on Billy Thomas or John Fairclough or Nigel Taylor and look really good. They're all as big as him and if he could prove superiority over them no-one would dare cross him. Why does he pick on me? Do you know?

I'm little and ugly and I've got big ears and a crooked nose and greasy hair and a square uniform and a huge satchel and a fussy mother and asthma and puny fists and I can't run as fast as him and anyone could win a fight with me – and most people do. What satisfaction does he get from taking my dinner money and ripping my clothes when it's so easy for him? Why don't *you* want to beat me up?

But who am I to complain? Nobody wants me, I'm useless except as a form of entertainment for the rest of the school. So Eddy Jones strides across the playground towards me and I shut my eyes and switch off my brain. The girls giggle and the boys cheer. His friends are ever so proud to be 'in' with Eddy Jones.

Friends? Friends full of awe and admiration, security and image but most of all fear and hatred. Will you be my friend? Really? You're the only real friend I've got – and that's one more than Eddy Jones has.

This school's a giant feudal system and I'm at the bottom. Eddy Jones is at the top. I'm the pawn and he is the king. But why? What gives him the right to rule?

They say that Eddy's Mum's gone away and his Dad doesn't care about him. They say his Dad gets drunk all the time and hits Eddy. They say his Dad spends all their money on booze. Maybe that's why Eddy's still wearing the same uniform he had in the first year.

Eddy's in the bottom class – and he doesn't go to that often. The girls all make fun of him and say he's thick – the boy's don't dare. The same girls call me a square and a swot just because I'm in the top set.

That's what's wrong with society, you have to be average. Individualism is a sin – you must be the average citizen or you're an outsider. To be a social success you have to be in the middle set with average grades. The same hair cut and clothes and accent as everyone else. The right colour, religion, shape, size and look. Who is the average citizen? Does he really exist?

Eddy and I are total opposites – yet we are alike in our differences. He thinks he is a total failure and I am a success – but we are both unhappy. We are ridiculed by the average society, rejected by our peers.

He hates me with a jealous fury. He knows he's not wanted by anyone and everyone hates him – but isn't a feeling of hatred better than no feelings at all?

There was a time when no-one had any feelings for us. We were nothing to them. We needed a purpose – something to be – something to be recognised for. We needed to be noticed.

So we found our places in this feudal system school. We are no longer outsiders but purposeful members for the average people to notice and watch – and maybe even care for.

He is Eddy Jones – school bully – and I am his plaything. These are the places in life which have captured the attention and feelings of the average people. We are needed and wanted so these are the places we'll keep by mutual understanding. My whinging questions and cries for help? They are just another way of milking sympathy from the average people. I even tried it with you didn't I? That's just the way I have grown to be.

I'm Eddy Jones's plaything – and I always will be.

Prayer

May we always try to treat people as we would like to be treated ourselves.

It might be suitable to introduce a source of help for anyone who is being bullied. There is a telephone number:
ChildLine on Freefone 0800 1111 or write to them at:
Freepost 1111, London N1 0BR or send a large stamped addressed envelope to:
Kidscape, World Trade Centre, Europe House, London E1 9AA

Acceptance

Reading

Accept Me for What I am by *Monica Dickens*

Accept me for what I am and I'll accept you for what you're accepted as.

from **Under the Eye of the Clock** by *Christy Nolan*

Let me introduce Christopher Nolan. He is 25 years old and is the author of two best selling books, the first published when he was 15 years old. He is a winner of the Whitbread Prize with his life story, *Under the Eye of the Clock*, and he has been hailed as a literary genius.

So what you may ask? Don't switch off, and I'll tell you what.

Christopher Nolan has never been able, all his life, to walk or talk or control his limbs.

His birth on September 6th 1965 was difficult and his brain was deprived of vital oxygen. The resulting brain damage left him incapable of speech or co-ordinated movement, BUT mentally unimpaired – his thinking and feeling was perfect.

This boy might have had no kind of life at all, perhaps shut away in an institution where no-one could ever guess what a brilliant intelligence was locked into his disabled body (later, one insensitive journalist called his mind a "diamond in a rubbish bin . . ."). His parents, Joe and Bernadette, were soon convinced that he was a bright child. They sang to him, read to him, taught him poetry, discussed everything with him, flooded speech into his speechless, eagerly receptive mind. So, ever since he was three he had been mentally writing poems, developing the muscles of his mind because all his other muscles were useless. His talented sisters danced and acted for him and he went to the pantomime. On camping holidays they held him in a mountain stream so that his cramped limbs could feel the delight of clear, cold water.

"His mother it was who treated him as normal, tumbled to his intelligence, tumbled to his eye-signal talk." (His own description.) Bernadette herself remembers a long ago day in the farmhouse kitchen. A visitor came in while she was clearing up, and she shoved a greasy roasting pan into the oven and forgot it. Days later, she turned on the oven to bake bread. Chris, then only two years old, became agitated, threw himself about and roared his baby noises more violently, as Bernadette opened the oven door on a sizzling cloud of black smoke.

Just once, he wept for his affliction, "He was only three years old, but he cried the tears of a sad man." With his eyes, he told his mother to listen to the birds, to children playing outside, and to look at his useless body. "Why, why, why me?"

Through his despairing tears she told him, "You can see, you can hear, you can think and understand everything you hear. Dad and I love you just as you are, and wherever we go, you'll come."

Burned for ever in his mind was the knowledge that he was accepted and now he could accept himself, and like himself. It was amazingly young to discover the key to joy and strength in living.

He shared everything with his family, but still he had no voice for the world, and he desperately longed to communicate his billowing, colourful thoughts and fantasies.

When he was seven it was time for schooling; the family left the farm and moved to Dublin where Chris became a pupil of the school attached to the Central Remedial Clinic. It was here that he made his first life long friend, Alex Clark, who took him everywhere and even played wheelchair football with him, dribbling the ball between the wheels as he pushed the chair. His occupational therapist, Eve Fitzpatrick, strapped a "unicorn stick" to his forehead and he tried to type, struggling against the violent, defeating spasms. Every word was a ten minute battle as he tried to jab at each letter on the typewriter with the stick fixed to his forehead.

When he was eleven a drug called Lioresal, a new treatment of cerebral palsy, steadied his head, and all his mind's treasure broke through in what he was to call a "dam-burst of dreams."

Bernadette put the typewriter on the kitchen table, and "cushioned his sad chin on her cosy cupped hands" watching in amazement as he "solemnly aimed his head-stick at the letters pouring into his mind" and he typed out a poem:

Polarized, I was paralysed
Plausibility palated,
People realized totally,
Woefully, once I totally
Opened their eyes.

His haunting, brilliant poems and short stories won top awards from the Spastics Society and he flew to London to acclaim and recognition.

"He plunges into language as if it were his escape route from death," wrote John Carey, Professor of English Literature at Oxford University. "An intense self floods out through his typewriter." Cambridge professor Christopher Ricks said: "He uses words as though he were passing electric shocks through a dead body."

Later, with his typical ability to laugh at himself, he wrote about the excitement: "Can you credit all of the fuss that was made of a cripple?" He uses the term "cripple" freely. It's no insult to him.

Welcomed by John Medlycott, the school's enlightened headmaster, Chris was able to move to Mount Temple, a large comprehensive. That took courage, and the support of new friends like Paul Browne and Helen Shail who championed him and protected him from the few jeering sceptics. The main boost to Chris's confidence was these good friends who gave him "love in bucketfuls."

When Paul Browne first met him in class, "We looked at each other with instant understanding. We worked out a code, and got up to all sorts of jokes and games with a crowd of other boys. Out behind the gym, having a quick smoke, we might hear some dumb kid only two yards away say, "That bloke is an eejit.""

"I'd tell Chris, 'Let's make a joke of it,' and we'd just laugh."

At home, he wrote and wrote. He typed beauty from within: "Brilliant, bright boiling words poured into his mind," and he "gimleted his words onto white sheets of life."

Small wonder, with his unique, arresting style, that his first book – Dam-Burst of Dreams, published in 1981 when he was 15 – brought him a deluge of publicity and praise.

After leaving school, Chris went to Trinity College, Dublin, for a year before deciding to devote all his time to writing. His autobiography was to be "the saga of helpless, crippled man . . . dashed, branded and treated as dross," and "how my brain-damaged life is as normal for me as my able-bodied friends' is for them."

'Under the Eye of the Clock', typed out laboriously and painfully, was published in 1987, gathering a Whitbread award and a wealth of praise for his talent, which many call genius. Reviewers compared him to James Joyce, Samuel Beckett, Dylan Thomas. Chris indicates the authors with a glance at the bookshelf, then shakes his head and looks down at himself: "My writing is ME."

In his autobiography, Chris wrote: "Accept me for what I am and I'll accept you for what you're accepted as." His intent blue eyes search your soul. With his fantastic sense of humour, he sees the joke before you do, and his nodding, disorganized head falls forward and flings back in gurgles of laughter and the energetic, expressive sounds which are his speech without words.

"You like yourself, Chris?"

His eyes flick up for "Yes". He looks at the ceiling, where God is. Yes to God. Yes to myself. "This is me."

In his sunny study at the front of the house, with the unicorn stick on his head and Bernadette cradling his chin, Christopher Nolan typed a special message to everyone like himself:

"Never compare your life to others. Try to look at what is positive within yourself. Beauty is but a tag, hope is far better and longer lasting. Love your own interior image and respect your soul's feeble joy. Remember too that you will never have to bear the burden of being 'Able-bodied', but the seeming fortunate may one day suddenly find themselves bearing the golden label – CRIPPLE."

Prayer

"Accept me for what I am and I'll accept you for what you're accepted as."

Christmas Time

Reading

Nativity Play by *Mary Buckley*

The great event of the primary school at this time of the year is the Nativity Play. Six and seven year olds have been rehearsing for weeks, their minds firmly fixed, one suspects, not so much upon Bethlehem and donkeys as Hollywood and Cadillacs.

There's the trauma of getting a part in the first place: being overlooked to play Joseph is bad enough for six year old Darren but to Darren's Mum it's probably worse than expulsion from the tennis club.

The other problem about the nativity play is the costumes. When I was at school it was easy. Joseph wore his dad's woollen striped dressing gown, Mary wore her mum's long white nightie and a blue curtain. All the wise men were dressed in flannelette sheets and all the shepherds had tea towels tied round their heads with dressing gown cords.

Somehow, it doesn't seem so easy now. All the fathers wear silk pyjamas, mothers are in lacy negligées. It's not quite so easy to convert a duvet cover into eastern robes and all the tea towels have "a present from Majorca" emblazoned across them, usually in dayglo colours.

The angels are still easy, crepe paper and tinsel. But the spiky hair styles make the conversion from Garry to Gabriel a little hard.

And the baby itself – there was always a little girl who had a chubby-cheeked baby doll. Her mother spent weeks preparing the white clothes, a little lace, some ribbon. Somehow, a cabbage patch doll or a teenage mutant hero turtle does not seem so . . . appropriate.

But, never mind. There they are, scrubbed faces shining, hair gleaming in the lights, word perfect on the night. The old carols haven't changed, Silent Night, Little Donkey, Away in a Manger, and although the piano is now replaced by a synthesiser, the story does not change. . . .

No Room at the Inn by *Dina Donohue*

Wallace Purling was nine that year and only in the second form. Most people in town knew that he had difficulty keeping up. He was big and clumsy, slow in movement and mind. Still, Wally was well liked by the other children in his class, though the boys had trouble hiding their irritation when Wally asked to play ball games with them.

Most often they'd find a way to keep him out, but Wally would hang around anyway – just hoping. He was a helpful boy, willing and smiling, and the natural protector of the under-dog. When the older boys chased the younger ones away, it was always Wally who said, "Can't they stay? They're no bother."

Wally fancied the idea of being a shepherd with a flute in the nativity play that Christmas, but the teacher in charge assigned him a more important role. The Innkeeper did not have many lines, and Wally's size would make his refusal of lodging to Joseph more forceful.

The usual large audience gathered for the yearly extravaganza. Wallace Purling stood in the wings, watching with fascination.

Then Joseph appeared – slowly, tenderly guiding Mary – and knocked hard on the wooden door, set into the painted backdrop.

"What do you want?" Wally the Inkeeper said brusquely, swinging the door open.

"We seek lodging."

"Seek it elsewhere," Wally looked straight ahead but spoke vigorously. "The inn is filled."

"Sir, we have asked everywhere in vain. We have travelled far and are weary."

"There is no room in the inn for you." Wally looked properly stern.

"Please, good Innkeeper, this is my wife, Mary. She is heavy with child. Surely you must have some small corner for her to rest?"

Now, for the first time, the Innkeeper looked down at Mary. There was a long pause, long enough to make the audience tense with embarrassment.

"No! Begone!" the prompt whispered from the wings.

"No!" Wally repeated. "Begone!"

Joseph sadly placed his arm round Mary. Mary laid her head upon her husband's shoulder and the two of them started to move away. Wally stood in the doorway, watching the forlorn couple. His mouth was open, his brow creased with concern, his eyes filling unmistakably with tears.

And suddenly this Christmas play became different from all others.

"Don't go, Joseph," Wally called out. "Bring Mary back." Wallace broke into a bright smile, "You can have *my* room."

A few thought the play had been ruined. Most considered it the best Christmas play they had ever seen.

Prayer

May we have room in our hearts for others, particularly at this time of the year.

Decisions

Reading

Where to from here? by *Zelpha Conway (aged 16)*

I have always had many people around me and I love other people's company but at the moment I have some very important decisions to make. I have to decide what college I'm going to and what courses to take and the career I want to follow. The problem is, I have people around me (the one's who stop me from feeling alone) who have expectations of me and I sometimes wonder if I can live up to them.

It is my dream to be a primary school teacher. I think it is a wonderful job – to think that a child comes into your class and can't read or write or spell or do sums and by the end of that year they can, because you've taught them to. At the primary school age the children are so eager to learn and achieve what they want to. I can imagine this job to be really rewarding. The thing is, I don't know if I could pass "A" levels and I can't get a teaching job without them.

My parents have always had high hopes for me and I've always managed to please them. One of them has wanted me to be a teacher since I was young and the thought only appealed to me in the last couple of years. My other parent wants the best for me too, but is not so forceful about it.

So, you see, I have these decisions to make and I'm finding it very hard to do the "right" thing. I feel so alone in my decisions because I feel that nobody understands how important this is for me. I'm sure I'm not the only one going through this right now though, and it's something I must sort out quickly before it's too late to apply for the college and courses I choose.

It's like being stuck in a prison cell and I can't get out without making my decisions. It's so difficult though because if I don't get my "A" levels then I'll feel so disappointed in myself and I'll have let down the people who love me – when I want them to be proud of me.

I fear in my heart and soul I won't achieve my ambition, but I so desperately want to be a primary school teacher that I'm willing to "go for it".

I am also dreading receiving my GCSE results, because if I don't get good grades, I won't be able to take the "A" levels. . . .

Still, I shall continue to work hard and, with a bit of luck too, maybe I will become a primary school teacher and I'm sure I shall be very happy.

Prayer

Making decisions can be very lonely and difficult. May we have the courage to use what talents we have wisely, and live this day to the full.

Giving

Reading

In 1984 a famine in Ethiopia was reported on the BBC News in a brief, but very graphic video. The report, by Michael Buerk, was broadcast to 470 million people on 425 of the world's networks and covered perhaps the most harrowing sights ever shown on television. Like living skeletons, famine victims too weak to stand raised match-stick-like arms in a silent plea for food. Mothers cradled their dying infants. A tearful young girl stared hauntingly through the window of a makeshift mortuary at the body of her two year old brother. . . .

The public reaction was enormous and led to several fund raising appeals. Perhaps the most colourful fund–raiser was Bob Geldof – an Irish rock star, lead singer of the Boomtown Rats. He was the driving force behind Band Aid and Live Aid.

The extract below describes his personal reaction to that television broadcast:

from **Is That It?** by *Bob Geldof*

It was coming to the end of 1984 and I could see no prospect for the release of an album the Boomtown Rats and I had sweated over and were proud of. All day I had been on the phone trying to promote a single from the album. I went home in a state of blank resignation and switched on the television. But there I saw something that placed my worries in a ghastly new perspective.

The news report was of famine in Ethiopia. From the first seconds it was clear that this was a horror on a monumental scale. The pictures were of people who were so shrunken by starvation that they looked like beings from another planet. Their arms and legs were as thin sticks, their bodies spindly. Swollen veins and huge, blankly staring eyes protruded from their shrivelled heads. The camera wandered amid them like a mesmerised observer, occasionally dwelling on one person so that he looked directly at me, sitting in my comfortable living room.

And there were children, their bodies fragile and vulnerable as premature babies but with the consciousness of what was happening to them gleaming dully from their eyes. All around was the murmur of death like a hoarse whisper, or the buzzing of flies.

From the first few seconds it was clear that this was a tragedy which the world had somehow contrived not to notice until it had reached a scale which constituted an international scandal. You could hear that in the tones of reporter Michael Buerk. It was the voice of a man who was registering despair, grief and disgust at what he was seeing. At the end the newscasters remained silent. Pauline, my wife, burst into tears, and then rushed upstairs to check our baby, Fifi, who was sleeping peacefully in her cot.

The images played and replayed in my mind. What could I do? Did not the sheer scale of the thing call for something more? Michael Buerk had used the word biblical: a famine of biblical proportions. A horror like this could not occur today without our consent. We had allowed this to happen. I would send money. But that was not enough. I was stood against the wall. I had to withdraw my consent. What else could I do? I was only a pop singer – and by now not a very successful pop singer. All I could do was make records that no one bought. But I would do that, I would give the profits of the next Rats record to Oxfam. What good would that do? It would be a pitiful amount. But it would be more than I could raise by simply dipping into my shrunken bank account. Maybe some people would buy it just because the profits were going to Oxfam. And I would withdraw my consent. Yet that was not enough.

Bob Geldof decided to make a new record – with a difference. Over the next few days he wrote the song "Do They Know It's Christmas," with fellow singer Midge Ure and spent hours on the telephone, cajoling top pop musicians into joining him in a special group, named Band Aid, to record it.

The disc was an instant hit and eventually sold 3.5 million. Together with the sale of T-shirts, photographs and videos of the record being made, a mammoth £8 million was raised.

However, it wasn't only the famous who reacted so generously. In Iver, Buckinghamshire, six-year-old Janet Joss loaded a pram with her toys and sold them door to door in the village – they fetched £40. Mr and Mrs Alec West of Mulben in Scotland auctioned all the china, glass and furniture they did not need in their home. The sale raised £2,430.

In Kent, a barber shaved ten people in four minutes – blindfolded – and raised £150. Throughout the length and breadth of the country people responded to the appeals – newspapers donated money and clothing contributed by their readers; factory workers in Yorkshire toiled without pay to prepare ten tons of high energy biscuits in time for an emergency flight to Ethiopia; dockers in Southampton ignored traditional demarcation rules to work alongside farmers over Christmas, loading 10,000 tonnes of wheat. Overtime payments were waived so thousands of pounds were saved.

The list is endless. Bob Geldof has continued with the vast fund–raising projects, but there is no happy ending to the story. Famine still ravages areas of the world. The technology of the 1990's does not bring a solution to the age old problem, but enables us to be aware of what is happening in the world at large. Oxfam Director Guy Stringer said at the time, "The response to the Ethiopian famine was by far the greatest of any charitable giving in our history. Oxfam has long been familiar with British generosity, but the depth of feeling behind these donations has awed me."

Prayer

May we be aware of what is happening in the world around us and let us help others whenever we can, by using whatever talents we may have.

Excuses

Reading

I wonder how many times you have had to make an excuse?
We've all done it at one time or another haven't we? Why do
we feel the need to "make excuses"? Sometimes we try to
wriggle out of trouble, sometimes we try to avoid having to do
something we do not like. Let me give you a couple of examples
and you'll know just what I mean. Humour can help to make an
excuse go with a real swing . . . .

A young man had just received a final warning from his boss about
being late for work. Soon after, he was caught in a traffic jam on his way
to work. He'd used the "Mum is not well" and "my great Aunt died" too
often and he decided that this type of excuse wouldn't work anymore.
Anyway, his boss was probably pacing up and down with a dismissal
speech rehearsed.

He was. When Sam entered the office at 9.35am everyone was hard at
work. His boss approached him. Suddenly, Sam forced a grin and put
out his hand.

"How do you do!" he said. "I'm Sam Maynard. I'm applying for a job
I understand became available just 35 minutes ago. Does the early bird
get the worm?"

The room exploded into laughter. Smothering a smile, the boss
walked back to his office. Sam Maynard had saved his job with the only
tool that could win – a laugh.

Not everybody can think so quickly and get away with using humour as
an excuse as well as that example. More often than not, the excuse you
compose sounds just right when you rehearse it, but it doesn't quite
come off when you apply it. The comedian Jasper Carrot tells of some
real examples taken from insurance forms where drivers have tried to
explain what has happened in an accident:

"Coming home I drove into the wrong house and collided with a tree
I don't have . . ."

"I knocked over a man. He admitted it was his fault as he had been knocked over before . . ."

"I told the police I was not insured but, on removing my hat, found I had a fractured skull . . ."

"The old fellow was all over the road. I had to swerve a number of times before I hit him . . ."

These excuses were used to try and make it appear that the accident was caused by someone else. They didn't really work because the truth was distorted and consequently the excuses sounded ridiculous.

Sometimes, when we make excuses, we are so busy trying to make things right for ourselves that we forget about the impact our actions may have on others. Listen to this story and see what I mean:

There was once a young man, John, who was away from home fighting in his country's war. Just before Christmas John wrote to his family about a friend who had had his legs blown off in a minefield. He explained that his friend was being drafted home as an invalid, and in his letter he asked his family to offer hospitality to his injured friend for Christmas.

When John's mother received the letter, she wrote the following reply:

'Thank you for your letter. We were terribly sorry to hear the news about your friend. We are making preparations for Christmas and, Son, you know how things are. Your Aunt is coming for a few days and I'm sure you understand our difficulties. We have only one bathroom and that is upstairs. You do understand, don't you, how awkward it would be for us? It's not that we don't want to help your friend, but can you explain to him that we can't take him at this time? Believe me, we *are* very sorry.'

Shortly after their son received this disappointing reply the enemy over-ran his camp. Many men were killed, including John. His grieving Mother asked that his body be flown home as she wanted the consolation of a family funeral. Her wish was granted and when the body arrived home she asked that she could see her son for the last time before he was buried.

When the coffin lid was lifted, she saw that John's legs had been blown off at the knees. . . .

We began by saying that we use excuses for many reasons – usually for our own ends, to get us out of some sort of difficulty. An African proverb sums it all up very clearly:

"One does not have to learn how to fall into a pit; all it takes is the first step, the others take care of themselves. . . ."

Prayer

Perhaps, in the future, before we start on elaborate excuses, we may stop and think. Then, we may not need to take that "first step".

Death

Reading

When the Cat's Away by *Bruce (aged 14)*

This is an account of a family and what happened to that family when one of the parents suddenly died.

"When the cat's away the mice can play". Well, that's what they say, isn't it? But what if the cat dies? That's another matter.

My life was just like most kids' lives, came home, expected dinner on the table, helped a little, not enough. My mother was taken for granted, expected to be there. My father was/is ruptured and an alcoholic. I think he drinks to ease the pain. He used to argue a lot with my mother.

We had/have a caravan. That was the only place my mother got away from work. We used to go up there weekends and school holidays. My mother and I had wonderful times there. I would try to get her out and she would come. She was the most wonderful person I have ever known. She was the only one I could discuss my problems with and I shared hers.

I used to go down to the beach most days. Either my mother would come with me or come later in the day. In the last year of her life, I was going out with a girl whom I had met while staying at the caravan. My mother liked the girl and she liked my mother. My mother never said anything bad about the girls I went around with.

It was the 5th of November. We were out in the garden and we were letting off our fireworks. My mother had just brought up some potatoes in their jackets. My mother had just been pruning some rose bushes when she fell ill all of a sudden. We took her upstairs. I went next door to call the doctor. I phoned, then came back. They told me to wait downstairs. I waited outside the house, leaning on the gate. I don't know why, but I was thinking what would happen if she died. I was standing there crying for what seemed like hours, then the doctor came. He gave her an injection and then phoned for an ambulance, which arrived quite quickly. They took her off to the hospital.

The next day my father went to see her. When he got back he said that she was all right. He rang up an hour later. He came in and told my brother and me that my mother was dead. I ran upstairs and started to cry as though I could never stop. At first I blamed it all on my father.

My grandmother on my mother's side was staying with us when all this happened. What with the funeral and all the other things that had to be done, everything got behind e.g. the washing and the housework. But we soon got organised. Everything was practically the same since my nan did the cooking. I just had to do a bit more work. But I have no one to take my problems to, no shoulder to cry on when I feel like a good sob.

But that doesn't matter any more. I've now learned to live with my problems. Well, what else could I do?

We get along fine, really. My brother and I still argue about everything. One day my nan and I had an argument in which my nan accused me of driving my mother to her death – not in so many words, though. I shouted something like, "If you ever say that again I'll kill you." I ran upstairs and threw myself on the bed. After about 15 minutes, she came and apologised to me. I'll never forgive her for that, whatever she does. That was the most wicked thing I've ever had done to me.

Recently, and in the near past, I have done things that I haven't wanted to do. Sometimes my brother makes my room in a mess – not wrecked, but little things just out of place which gets on my nerves. When he has gone out, I take it out on myself. I actually have fits. As you come through the front door there's a dent in the right hand side of the wall where I banged my own head against it. Then the kitchen door is smashed where I kicked it. Sometimes I wish I could leave home but there is nowhere to go. I often think of suicide and then I say no. It would be too painful and, anyway it would mean defeat for me. Why should I please so many people?

If anyone reading this knew me, they would have realised that this is the inner me speaking and not the me they might have seen. The outer me is happy and mad and was made for me to hide behind. This personality is much nicer than the other personality. I have found that nearly all the people I have met have a second personality, like me, behind which they can hide.

The death of a member of one's family is devastating and Bruce has described his feelings so that we can understand why he should, at one moment, feel resentment and the next, deep loss. He says that he gets along "fine" and he has had to learn to cover his sadness, but the emptiness and missing the nearness of his mother is still very real for him.

I wonder what you think of these thoughts by Canon Scott Holland? They were written to comfort people in a situation like that of Bruce and give us a very different idea about death:

"Death is nothing at all . . . I have only slipped away into the next room . . . I am I and you are you . . . , whatever we were to each other, that we are still. Call me by my old familiar name, speak to me in the easy way which you always used. Put no difference into your tone; wear no forced air of solemnity or sorrow. Laugh as we always laughed at the little jokes we enjoyed together. Play, smile, think of me, pray for me. Let my name be ever the household word that it always was. Let it be spoken without an effort, without the ghost of a shadow on it. Life means all that it ever meant. It is the same as it ever was; there is absolutely unbroken continuity. What is this death but a negligible accident? I am but waiting for you, for an interval, somewhere near, just around the corner."

Prayer

For a few moments, let us think about the two readings we have heard this morning. Perhaps the feelings expressed in each of them may help us, and those we love, in the future.

Old Age (1)

Reading

My Aunt by *Nina Denton (aged 16)*

Her face was gaunt, her skin white, thin and shiny. The last time we had visited her in this hospital ward, her eyes had still darted about with a little flicker of enthusiasm, although they were clouded with discomfort. This evening she dozed, impatient, waiting for death. Her eyes were closed, she drew in breath fitfully through an oxygen mask. The valve of the oxygen canister rattled, the breaths jerked and bubbled in her throat.

First my aunt had lived in a flat near a railway line; then she moved to Bedford. We visited her there every so often. The flat was near a river. The radiators were always on full blast and pots of geraniums stood on the window sills giving off a damp, peppery stench. My Aunt said that the secret of the success of her geraniums was the fact that she spoke to them and gave them tea leaves. The walls of the rooms were white and sparse and several of her paintings were propped up against them. We sat on her squashy, uncomfortable sofa and perched plates of bread and cheese and spring onions on our laps. She'd tell us about the time when she had had shingles and struggled with her shopping trolley in Sainsbury's; about the Christmas party which she always attended at the local prison. We'd look at the paintings she'd done and admire the strange drawings of flowers. The conversation never wavered. Then, in the late afternoon we would drive back home again, past stinking brick kilns and through the only village in England with a green telephone box.

I can remember her voice even now, her chuckle and the way she exclaimed, "Oh Gawd!" in her slight London accent when she was joking about how awful people were. She had been born in Chelsea. I knew little of her past – it was as mysterious as her paintings which puzzled me greatly. They were strange landscapes jumbled with portraits, creeping plants that turned into writhing snakes, flowers and birds that looked like faces from another angle and strange eyes that peered through the vegetation. These creatures came entirely from her imagination. Once she had been treated for mental illness. They gave her electro-convulsive therapy.

Her eyes were blue, quick and intelligent. Her nose was slightly hawk–like. She was very moderately plump and she wore the sort of square-toed shoes generally attributed to old people. Mad she was not, unconventional perhaps, and misunderstood. My Aunt had a desire to wander and could never settle or be happy in one place. It was always time to move on. She had, apparently, even considered becoming a tramp! Once they made her go to a Day Centre where she was forced to cut out bits of paper and make childish collages. She was married once, but the marriage had been unhappy. In any case, the man had long since died.

She liked purple. There was mauve toilet paper in the bathroom, she was fond of purple irises and indeed often wore the colour herself. She used to take long walks by the river, but gradually went less and less. Eventually, she moved to another flat, the size of a shoe box in the centre of Bedford. It was depressingly grim. There was a view of a small patch of grass over which a washing line was strung and terraced houses stretched as far as the eye could see. It was a hot, dusty summer's day and she was imprisoned in this flat. She was having problems with her lungs and couldn't walk far enough to escape the claustrophobic maze of red brick and tarmac. Her stay in this place didn't last long. She soon moved into another home, her last, excluding the hospital. It was a large house in Northwood, converted into a retirement home. The residents were mainly middle class women who sat sipping tea in a refined manner in the lounge. My Aunt got a pretty rough deal. Her room was a tiny segment of another room, roughly partitioned off with board. There was just enough space to accommodate a wardrobe, a bed, a few chairs and a rusty oxygen canister prescribed to her by a doctor. There was a view over a garden, which she seldom visited. She never quite fitted in at the home. The other residents were too snobbish, she was too lively to appeal to their dull senses of humour. My Aunt told us the story of when she first came there and sat down in an armchair in the lounge. "You can't sit there. That's my seat!" a woman said to her. That was the sort of people they were.

She was admitted to hospital. At first she was in a barrack-like ward, a long rectangular room with a flickering television set at one end. Then she was moved to another ward because the barrack-like buildings were to be knocked down. I think I saw her twice in that last ward. The first time she spoke a little from underneath the oxygen mask. The last time I just held her papery hand, as light as a sparrow's skeleton.

Prayer

In our busy lives, may we make time to be aware of the needs of people around us, particularly those less fortunate than ourselves.

Old Age (2)

Reading

A Crabbit Old Woman

A poem found in an elderly woman's bedside locker after she died in a geriatric hospital. In it, she describes her deepest feelings, her memories and she asks that the people around, caring for her, should also "see" her. Although her body is old and her reactions are slow, her mind is still sensitive to love. She wishes that she could be seen as her life has been and not just the Crabbit Old Woman she appears now to be.

What do you see, nurses, what do you see?
Are you thinking when you look at me –
A crabbit old woman, not very wise,
Uncertain of habit with far-away eyes.
Who dribbles her food and makes no reply,
When you say in a loud voice "I do wish you'd try".
Who seems not to notice the things that you do
And forever is losing a stocking, a shoe.
Who unresisting or not lets you do as you will
With bathing and feeding, the long day to fill.
Is that what you're thinking? Is that what you see?
Then open your eyes, nurse, you are not looking at me.

I'll tell you who I am as I sit here so still
As I rise at your bidding, as I eat at your will.
I'm a small child of ten with a father and mother;
Brothers and sisters who love one another;
A young girl of sixteen with wings on her feet
Dreaming that soon now a lover she'll meet;
A bridge soon at twenty my heart gives a leap
Remembering the vows that I promised to keep.

At twenty-five now I have young of my own
Who need me to build a secure happy home;
A woman of thirty, my young now grow fast,
Bound to each other with ties that should last.

At forty my young sons now grown, will be gone;
But my man stays beside me to see I don't mourn;
At fifty once more babies play around my knee.
Again we know children, my loved one and me;
Dark days are upon me, my husband is dead
I look to the future, I shudder with dread.

My young are all busy rearing young of their own.
And I think of the years and the love that I've known.
I'm an old woman now and Nature is cruel,
'Tis her jest to make old age look like a fool.
The body it crumbles, grace and vigour depart.
There is now a stone where I once had a heart.

But inside this old carcase a young girl still dwells
And now and again my battered heart swells.
I remember the joys, I remember the pain,
And I'm loving and living all over again.
And I think of the years all too few – gone too fast
And accept the stark fact that nothing will last.
So open your eyes, nurses, open and see,
Not a crabbit old woman, look closer – see me!

Prayer

Help us to open our eyes and see . . .

Sometimes it happens

Reading

And sometimes it happens that you are friends and then
You are not friends,
And friendship has passed.
And whole days are lost and among them
A fountain empties itself.

And sometimes it happens that you are loved and then
You are not loved,
And love is past.
And whole days are lost and among them
A fountain empties itself into the grass.

And sometimes you want to speak to her and then
You do not want to speak,
Then the opportunity has passed.
Your dreams flare up, they suddenly vanish.

And also it happens that there is nowhere to go and then
There is somewhere to go,
Then you have bypassed.
And the years flare up and are gone,
Quicker than a minute.

So you have nothing.
You wonder if these things matter and then
As soon as you begin to wonder if these things matter
They cease to matter,
And caring is past.
And a fountain empties itself into the grass.

by Brian Patten.

And Even Friends Lost be Friends Regained
by *Suzanne Cole (aged 16)*

I'm the type of person who likes to have friends around me and share lots of good times with other people. I can be quite jolly and cheerful, although, on the other hand, I can be serious, very deep thinking and intimate. I suppose that sums up my character quite well, seeing I am a Gemini star-sign. I most certainly live up to that expectation. My attitude can change just like the wind or at the snap of someone's fingers. I can go from "nice old Susie" to "spiteful and cold-hearted Susie" and it is this second side that has over-come me on a few occasions.

One incident which I am writing about involved myself and another ex-friend.

I enjoyed being in this person's company – it was fun and a laugh. However, soon and very quickly a serious, deep relationship developed. In fact, it was so quick that neither of us expected it to happen. I had good friendships at school with my other mates, but soon I let all that disappear into thin air when I abandoned them to be with this close friend. It soon developed into a situation where the two of us would see each other every day and every evening. We spent as much time together as we possibly could, never having time for our other friends, just thinking about each other. We were being selfish, but at the time we couldn't see how much we were hurting our other friends and they were too polite to say anything.

Anyway, the relationship between us both became very strong. It seemed as if nobody could ever break the bond between us. By now our other friends had had enough of settling for second best and being used. So, we lost all contact with them. From this situation we became very dependent upon each other, which, in turn, led to a lot of rows and disputes over silly things. We stuck together because we thought we knew what we were doing – "headstrong" was what they said. Our ex-friends excluded us from all the usual activities and conversations because they were annoyed at our behaviour.

Later on, the relationship between my friend and me began to slide downhill – we realised that we needed friends and we could not survive in an emotional vacuum. If a row took place we had no one to talk to about it and we realised that it is always easier to talk to friends than parents about personal emotions. After a slow and rocky few weeks, the close relationship ended. It was at that time I desperately needed someone to talk to and I had no one. From that day I said to myself that I must apologise to all the people I had hurt and neglected by the involvement with that one person.

It took a long time to get back in with my friends but I managed it. I felt so bad about the way I had treated my friends and if I had realised it at the time, I would never have acted in the way I did . . . As the saying goes, "You learn from your mistakes" and I most certainly did. It may well sound all rosy and cheerful now – it almost is – except that the relationship I had with my close friend became nasty and cruel. My attitude changed for I turned bitter and cruel. I had no feelings and I deliberately hurt my ex-friend on a number of occasions. Even now, I still row a lot with this person because, although we cannot stand being with each other, we cannot bear the thought of anyone else having the other person. We have tried so hard to have a relationship based on friendship, but we get too jealous of each other and this results in hurtful arguments. If only we could both understand the way each other feels, then maybe we could solve the problem. Until that day comes, we will both carry on the way we are – making up and breaking up. It is a shame, though, because we both once had something very special and the relationship between us was love. I suppose it still hurts even now because we both experienced our first real love at that time.

It is obvious now that I am writing about an ex-boyfriend, but I feel a lot clearer in my own state of mind by being able to express how I feel about past experiences, especially intimate ones, on paper. It is something I have never done before.

Through all this, there is one lesson I have learnt. A relationship between a girl and boy should not be so involved that you exclude your friends. You will always need friends (and they you) so be careful to cherish your friends and do not reject them for the sake of that one intense relationship. Before you know it, you could leave it too late to make amends. I can now say just how lucky I really was in that situation. If nothing else came from my experience, then I now appreciate and value my friends more than ever and I thank them for their patience with me as I went through my "horrid" time.

Prayer

The title of that piece of writing is "And even Friends Lost may be Friends Regained". Let us, in a quiet moment, think about our friends, how we treat their friendship and how they treat us.

Prejudice (1)

Reading

"Baby, we have no choice of what color we're born or who our parents are or whether we're rich or poor. What we do have is some choice over what we make of our lives once we're here. . . ."
from: **Roll of Thunder, Hear My Cry** by *Mildred Taylor*.

"Roll of Thunder, Hear My Cry" is a powerful and moving book based on the experience of the author's own family. The story was set in Mississippi of the 1930's, which was a hard place for a black child to grow up in. Mildred Taylor received the Newbery Medal for the book and when she accepted the Award she described how, during the 1950's, her family would pay an annual visit to their old home in the South. This is what she said:

As a small child I loved the South. I used to look forward with eager anticipation to the yearly trips we took there when my father would pack the car and my mother would fry chicken, bake a cake and sweet-potato pies, stir up jugs of ice water and lemonade, and set them all in a basket on the back seat of the car between my sister and me. In my early years the trip was a marvellous adventure, a twenty-hour picnic that took us into another time, another world; down dusty red roads and across creaky wooden bridges into the rich farm country of Mississippi, where I was born.

And life was good then. Running barefoot in the heat of the summer sun, my skin darkening to a soft, amber hue; chasing butterflies in the day, fireflies at night; riding an old mule named Jack and a beautiful mare named Lady; even picking a puff or two of cotton – there seemed no better world. And at night when neighboring relatives would gather and sit on the moonlit porch or by the heat of the fire, depending on the seasons, talk would turn to the old people, to friends and relatives who then seemed to have lived so long ago. As the storytellers spoke in animated voices and enlivened their stories with movements of great gusto, I used to sit transfixed, listening, totally engrossed. It was a magical time.

Yet even magical times must end.

I do not remember how old I was when the stories became more than tales of faraway people, but rather, reality. I do not remember when the twenty-hour picnic no longer was a picnic, the adventure no longer an adventure. I only remember that one summer I suddenly felt a climbing nausea as we crossed the Ohio River into Kentucky and was again admonished by my parents that my sister and I were now in the South and must remain quiet when we pulled into gas stations, that we must not ask to use the restrooms, that they would do all the talking.

That summer and the summers to come I grew to realize that the lovely baskets of food my mother always packed for the trips, she prepared because we could not eat in the restaurants; that the long overnight ride was because we could not sleep in motels; that the jugs of water and lemonade were because we could not drink the water at the fountains – at least not the fountains marked "White Only", which were usually newer and cleaner. I was to learn the fear of the police siren. I was to learn to hate the patrol-men who frisked my father and made him spread-eagle – all because of thirty-five miles per hour. I was to learn the terror of the back road and the long, long wait for morning while my father, exhausted from the drive, tried to sleep as my mother watched guard.

Prayer

In "Roll of Thunder, Hear My Cry" Mama says that we have some choice over what we make of our lives. She then says, "I pray to God you'll make the best of yours . . ." Let us reflect on her thoughts and what we have just heard.

Prejudice and Pride

Reading

A story by Alison White

So the first day of term had arrived at last. Ann Benson's face was pulled into a tight frown as she secured 11-year-old Katy's light brown hair into a beautiful pony tail.

"Here we are, a high one. Feel." Carefully, gently, she guided Katy's hands to the back of her head.

"That's about right," Katy grinned happily. "How do I look, Mum?"

"Fine." Ann, looking at her daughter, gulped away the hard lump forming in her throat. "Just fine – a proper schoolgirl. There's just enough time to feed Sabre now, and then we'll be off."

"I'll feed her," Katy smiled and carefully walked out of the room, feeling her way. "Then that way I can say goodbye to her at the same time."

Ann watched her daughter leave the room. The house was completely familiar territory to her and Katy could find everything she needed, but now, for the first time in her life, she would be totally alone at the new school.

Sabre was Katy's dog. She wasn't a guide dog – Katy was too young for one – but when she was 18, hopefully she would be allowed one. But, for now, Sabre, carefully trained by Katy's father, was her eyes. Sabre had a gentle temperament and loved children. Ann knew that Sabre was devoted to her young mistress and that Katy felt safest of all when Sabre was with her.

The primary school in the village was very small and the headteacher had kindly allowed Katy's dog to accompany her to school – a very special dispensation. Ann and her husband were grateful – but, because of this, Katy had become even more dependent on Sabre. Ann had known that once Katy was older, they would either have to travel miles to a special school for the blind, or Katy would have to manage on her own.

"It'll seem funny without Sabre," mused Katy, now ready for school with her coat on. "I hope they find someone nice to show me around, don't you Mum?" Someone who didn't feel lumbered, thought Ann. "I'm sure they will. But we'd better hurry up now or you'll be late. And we don't want to make a bad impression on your first day, do we?"

As they walked along to the school, Katy stumbled on a raised paving stone. Instinctively, Ann reached out to help her, but then she drew back. This was something that was bound to happen over the next few days, while Katy got used to being by herself. She would have to learn to cope with it alone. She, Ann, must not interfere.

"Mum?" Katy said, so questioningly. "Why didn't you help me?"

How could you explain to a child that you were trying to help her? Ann tried to reassure her. "You might find this happens – there might not always be someone with you."

"Other people will help me surely, Mum, won't they?" Katy didn't understand. The rest of the walk was in silence, with Katy troubled by what had happened. A part of Ann wanted to turn back and go straight home, although the voice of her conscience told her she had to prepare Katy for the outside world. The more preparation she had for it, the better able she'd be to face it.

When Ann arrived back home after leaving Katy at the school, she wondered if she was, after all, making life unnecessarily difficult for her daughter? But then she and her husband would not always be around. Hard though it was, Katy ought to have some independence. At least they were lucky to have the opportunity of sending her to an ordinary school. The nearest special schools were miles away.

For the first couple of weeks it seemed to be working beautifully. Katy seemed blissfully happy. She came home each night full of news about the day and then Ann began to notice a change in her. She was wary of answering questions about what she'd done during the day and was very quiet in the evenings. Too quiet – instead of chattering, she would just sit quietly, reading one of her Braille books.

When Ann heard Katy crying in bed one night, she went to her and tried to coax out of her what was wrong. Reluctant at first, Katy finally told her that one of the bigger girls had been making fun of her for not being able to see.

"Does she hurt you?" asked Ann, horrified and unable to believe that another child could be so unbearably cruel.

"Oh no." Katy seemed surprised at the suggestion. "She just tells me to come and look at things and then laughs because she knows that I can't see."

"How many of them treat you like this?"

"Only Janet Hargreaves and her friends. Everyone else is nice. Suzanne, my best friend, tells me not to take any notice. They laugh at her as well, but she's got used to it. Suzanne's mum has told her she's just got to take pride in herself."

"She's right," agreed Ann thoughtfully, but perhaps she should just have a quiet word with the headteacher about the situation.

As though reading her mind, Katy broke in, "Oh don't say anything, Mum!" and she turned to Ann pleadingly.

"All right," Ann sighed. "But you just tell Janet that the next time she says something like that, that you *can't* see, and will she describe whatever it is to you – and if she still bothers you after that then tell me."

Her advice seemed to do the trick and after a few days Katy was back to her old cheerful self and came home full of news of the things she and Suzanne had been doing. Pleased that Katy had found a real friend, Ann suggested she should ask Suzanne to tea one evening. Katy was thrilled at the idea, but came home from school next day tearful and upset.

Slowly, she explained that Suzanne's mother had said that she couldn't come to tea and had even wondered if they should be such close friends. She'd told Suzanne that together they were more of a target for the other girls. Bewildered by this, and with Katy unable to offer any further explanation, Ann suggested that she would like to meet Suzanne's mother and asked Katy to send a message to her via Suzanne.

So, two days later, Ann walked into the coffee bar where she'd arranged to meet Suzanne's mother. Then a tall, elegant woman walked over to her.

"Mrs Benson? I'm so pleased to meet you. I'm Sheena Carvell, Suzanne's mother. Shall we sit down?" she said, smiling.

With a sinking heart and a feeling of deep sadness, Ann sank into the seat. Katy hadn't understood why they taunted her friend: she, unspoilt and innocent, was unaware of any difference between her friend and the other girls – because of course she couldn't see the fine, proud features Suzanne had inherited from her beautiful West Indian mother.

Prejudice (2)

Reading

A Little Bit Nervous by *Elizabeth Eckford*
Elizabeth Eckford was one of nine black students who tried to enter the all white Little Rock Central High School in 1957. This is her account of what happened on that day.

Before I left home Mother called us into the living-room. She said we should have a word of prayer. Then I caught the bus and got off a block from the school . . .

At the corner I tried to pass through the long line of guards around the school. One of the guards pointed across the street. So I pointed in the same direction and asked whether he meant for me to cross the street and walk down. He nodded "yes". So, I walked across the street conscious of the crowd that stood there, but they moved away from me.

For a moment all I could hear was the shuffling of their feet. Then someone shouted, "Here she comes, get ready!" I moved away from the crowd on the sidewalk and into the street. If the mob came at me I could then cross back over so the guards could protect me.

The crowd moved in closer then began to follow me, calling me names. I still wasn't afraid. Just a little bit nervous. Then my knees started to shake all of a sudden and I wondered whether I could make it to the center entrance a block away. It was the longest block I ever walked in my whole life.

Just then the guards let some white students go through . . . I walked up to the guard who had let the white students in. He . . . didn't move.

When I tried to squeeze past him, he raised his bayonet and then the other guards closed in and they raised their bayonets. The crowd . . . moved closer and closer. Somebody started yelling, "Lynch her! Lynch her!"

I tried to see a friendly face somewhere in the mob – someone who maybe would help. I looked into the face of an old woman and it seemed a kind face, but when I looked at her again, she spat on me.

They came closer, shouting, "No nigger bitch is going to get in our school. Get out of here!"

I turned back to the guards but their faces told me I wouldn't get help from them. Then I looked down the block and saw a bench at the bus stop. I thought, "If I can only get there I will be safe."

When I finally got there, I don't think I could have gone another step. I sat down and the mob crowded up and began shouting all over again. Someone hollered, "Drag her over to this tree! Let's take care of the nigger." Just then a white man sat down beside me, put his arm around me and patted my shoulder. He raised my chin and said, "Don't let them see you cry."

Then a white lady – she was very nice – she came over to me on the bench. She spoke to me but I don't remember now what she said. She put me on the bus and sat next to me. She asked me my name and tried to talk to me but I don't think I answered . . . The next thing I remember I was standing in front of the School for the Blind, where Mother works . . . I ran upstairs, and . . . I kept running until I reached Mother's classroom.

Mother was standing at the window with her head bowed, but she must have sensed I was there because she turned around. She looked as if she had been crying, and I wanted to tell her I was all right. But I couldn't speak. She put her arms around me and I cried.

Prayer

Let us conclude by thinking about the words of an old African proverb:
"Three things are important in this world:
Good health
Peace with one's neighbour
Friendship with all . . ."

Last Lesson

Reading

BBC Thought for the Day Friday 18th October 1974 by
Colin M. Morris

There are any number of modern translations of the Bible on the bookstalls, but one still remains to be written. It isn't the Bible many of us profess to believe in, but the one we actually live by. Like any respectable Bible it would begin at Genesis, but it would be a sort of Genesis in reverse.

I quote: In the end, Man systematically dismantled the planet God had created. Being clever but not very wise, Man sized up the beautiful earth which was God's gift to him and said, "This land's worth at least a thousand quid an acre for development, and as for those useless animals roaming across it, their skins should fetch a fair amount." So Man did the unthinkable and sold his Mother, the Earth, and needlessly slaughtered his brothers and sisters of the animal kingdom. And his silly mate preened herself in their skins and furs. And this was the seventh day from the End.

And Man polluted the crystal-clear air with the fumes of his machines and poisoned the sea with garbage and turned rivers into foaming torrents of chemical waste and lakes into putrid rubbish tips. And Man began slowly, ever so slowly to choke himself to death. And this was the sixth day from the End.

And Man flexed his muscles, glorying in his strength. The powerful he called Great and those who sought only to serve others "weaklings" and "compromisers". And Man used his power to divide those who thought as he did from those who thought differently. The former he named allies and the latter, enemies. And he matched his strength against that of his enemies and challenged them to overcome him if they dared. And this was the fifth day from the End.

And Man said: the strong are entitled to most of what's going and the weak can have the rest. And he built great walls and recruited massive armies and equipped them with the weapons of terrifying destruction to protect his wealth. And so enchanted was he by the martial music of his tanks and jets and rockets that he was deaf to the pleas of the poor which turned in time to a terrible anger. And this was the fourth day from the End.

And Man slept uneasily, haunted in his dreams by the ghosts of those he had exploited. And he awoke afraid and set to work inventing the ultimate weapon. "Now," he said, "I feel safe." But his enemy did not, so he too created an ultimate weapon. And both lived under the shadow of extinction and called it peace. And this was the third day from the End.

And Man, swollen with pride and intoxicated by his achievements, said, "Let us make God in our own image, speaking our language and thinking our thoughts after us. And let our will become his will and our enemies his enemies and let us gaze into a mirror and worship the God we see there." And this was the second day from the End.

And Man stifled all truth that was not his own truth and called it propaganda, and he scoffed at the warnings of the prophets and silenced the ominous sounds of the earth in torment. And he averted his eyes from all that was unpleasant to behold and painful to watch. Instead, he gazed with delight upon the gleaming products of his ingenuity and he cried, "Bigger! Faster! Stronger! Richer! Louder! Higher! More!" And he became frantic with a desire nothing could satisfy. And that was the day before the End.

And the last day was chaos and noise and uproar and when the din subsided, Man and all his doings were no more. And the ravished Earth rested on the Seventh Day.

And then God spoke. "What a tragic waste! What a marvel was Man! He wasn't without courage and valour. He did some beautiful things and made some beautiful sounds. And he showed love and sacrifice and heroism."

And God turned and asked, "Well, what do *you* think? After all, you were there."

And Jesus said, "Let's try again."
Here endeth the last lesson.

Prayer

In a moment or two of quiet, let us individually consider what we have just heard.

Patience

Reading

The Black Raven, a fable by *Tayyiba Mussa (aged 16)*

The mother had died after giving birth to a beautiful son. She had died in peace knowing that her life had been meaningful and she had been happy with her husband. She also knew that the child she had given life to would be cherished and loved and properly cared for.

Four years on, the child had grown into a fine, healthy young boy. One day, when the father and son were out in the fields, the young boy, Ingar, spotted a black bird swaying to and fro. The father, busy sowing the second crop, always kept his eye on his son.

"Look, father! Look at that black bird!"

"Yes, Ingar, that's a raven."

A few minutes later, Ingar again said, "Look father! Look at that black bird."

Again, the father replied, "Yes, son."

Whenever Ingar saw another raven he exclaimed, "Look, father, at the black bird!" The father would always respond favourably. Ingar, fascinated by the raven, kept drawing his father's attention to the great bird. Not once did the father scold or reprimand his son for repeating the same thing. Instead, he made excuses for Ingar – his vocabulary was limited, he was fascinated with the flying black bird, he was learning – anything would excuse Ingar's actions. Ingar was loved dearly and the father never sent him away when the boy had a question. He would always give some explanation, a reason, an answer, whatever was required.

Ingar's father was not wealthy, but he was rich in heart and generous. He always hoped that Ingar would be satisfied with whatever life had to offer.

Twenty years later, Ingar had grown into a fine young man, educated socially as well as academically. He was newly married to a respectable girl. The father approved of this marriage, hoping that the girl would keep Ingar happy. Ingar's father was now ageing and lived with Ingar.

It was now Ingar's turn to look after and fend for his father and he did so quite well.

One day, Ingar's father received an invitation to a dinner being hosted by one of his childhood friends. He was pleased he'd been remembered and quite excited about seeing his old friend again. He was also excited about dressing up for the dinner. He noted the time: Thursday at 7.00pm. "That's about one week from today!" he thought and immediately started making plans – what he was going to wear, what he would talk about, how he would get there . . . He was like a child again! He kept reminding Ingar that he had a dinner to go to on Thursday at seven o'clock and that Ingar would have to drop him there. Ingar was told this *at least* three times a day, until the day arrived.

By Thursday, Ingar's father had bought, wrapped and re-wrapped the present for his old friend. By five o'clock in the evening he was dressed, ready and waiting with his present tucked under his arm.

"Ingar, I have to be there at seven o'clock. I don't want to be late. Do hurry up!"

"Father, it's just five o'clock and it's only a twenty minute drive from the house. We'll leave at 6.30pm, and you'll have lots of time to spare. Don't worry, you won't be late, I promise."

Ingar was getting slightly agitated. He had been hearing about this dinner ever since the invitation had arrived. It was as though nothing else was happening and "the dinner" was the most important event in the world.

"Ingar, son, what is the time? I don't want to be late."

"It's almost quarter past five. We have plenty of time."

Ten minutes later, Ingar's father again enquired about the time. Ingar gave him the time and returned to reading his newspaper. A few minutes later, "What's the time now, Ingar?" Ingar gave him the time and went back to the first paragraph in the newspaper. Every few minutes Ingar was interrupted, and by six o'clock he was really irritated.

"Ingar, what is the time now? Can we go now?"

Ingar, who didn't like being interrupted frequently when reading the newspaper and whose patience was now stretched to the utmost, snapped at his father, "You have been asking me the same question over and over again, every five minutes! I told you that we'd leave at 6.30pm. By asking what time it is every five minutes isn't going to make the time pass away any faster you know! Now, will you please let me get on with my reading!" Realising his harsh words and tone of voice, Ingar continued softly, "We will leave at six thirty. I promise you we will have plenty of time to spare."

Ingar's father who was taken aback with the young man's words – words he would not have expected of his son – felt sad. He realised that Ingar did not give much importance to "the dinner" and that Ingar did not realise how much the harsh words had hurt him.

"My son, I am sorry for being so irritating, but this dinner means a lot to me, and I hope I am excused. There is something I feel you ought to know. So, Ingar's father related the "Black Raven" incident to him, ending with, "I put up with your repetitiveness brought about with your fascination, without even one word of reprimand. I feel the harsh words that I just received were unfair and very selfish."

Ingar's face fell, knowing how much his father loved him and how much he had sacrificed for Ingar's sake. Now that he was older, Ingar's father lacked good memory and was very forgetful. There was nothing that would excuse Ingar's behaviour and he felt very sorry. He asked the forgiveness of his father, promising never to treat him like that again. "I'd rather die – please forgive me."

Ingar's father was pleased with this outcome and took Ingar into his arms. "Next time, we'll think of the 'Black Raven' before saying hasty words."

Prayer

Let us remember to *offer patience* in our dealings with others and may we also *receive patience* from others when we need it.

Values

Reading

Val's Perfect Crime by *Elizabeth Stucley*

"I've just got to have a bike," said Val to himself during the first week of the Easter holidays. "If I had a bike I could get out of this dump and away from Shorty's gang and go fishing and exploring, and see the world."

But the question was, how to get the money? Now Mum was not working, cash was shorter than usual. There had been no pocket money at all lately.

He tried the newsvenders, but they all had boys. Then he went along to see Mr Copley at the stationer's. But everyone knew Val's reputation.

"You're a bad lad," said old Mr Copley, looking at him over the top of his spectacles. Everyone says so. Always fighting!"

"I don't want to fight," muttered Val, standing sideways to hide a black eye that was fading all too slowly.

"Then why do you do it?" asked the old shopman. "Look at your coat! It's all ripped. And not a button on it. I want a smart lad."

Val turned up his arm. The lining stuck out of the cloth. Mum had practically given up mending for him. "It's a waste of my time," she had said. "You ought to go round painted blue like the savages."

"If the boy you've got now goes, would you take me on then?" asked Val.

"No. I want a steady boy," said Old Copley and turned away.

Val could not explain that he wanted to be steady, that he hated fighting. No one would have believed him. Then, he was proud, too proud to make excuses for himself. So he rubbed his nose on the back of his hand, and so transferred another smudge of black to his face. Dirt just grew on Val.

Next he tried the grocer's and the laundry.

"Don't you want a Saturday boy?" he asked. "I'll come evenings, too."

But they all declared they had boys and the laundry woman cried, "Go home and wash your face before you go asking for a job."

Val hadn't thought of that, so he stood there, taken aback.

The woman sniggered. "Tell your Mum to put you in the next bag wash."

Being laughed at was too much. Val could feel tears pricking in his eyes, so he ran away with the giggling of the laundry girls still in his ears.

At last he gave up his search for work, and went dawdling out into the yard. "It's enough to drive you to crime," he said to himself. "'Tisn't as if I wasn't wanting to earn some money honestly."

He went off across the Common and down the High Street. He scrumped an apple off a stall, not because he was hungry but as a revenge on a society that did not want him. He went and looked at the lovely, shining new bicycles in the shop windows. They had gears, pumps, shining bells, carriers – just everything. Val stood there imagining himself coasting down hills, racing along to the sea. And he said to himself, "It's not fair."

He began to hate everybody, and to feel the whole world was against him. He hated a community that refused to let him even work for a bicycle. Wandering on, he came to the Supermarket where there was a great crowd of people doing their shopping. They were pressed right up against the stalls, trying to attract the sellers' attention.

He watched a fat lady in a nylon fur coat. She had collected some bananas and a pineapple and was holding them out to be packaged. For a moment she had put down her purse on the counter amongst a bin of apples. Scarcely thinking, but acting on impulse, Val picked up the purse, pocketed it, and dived away out of the crowd. It was done in a second and he was out of sight before the woman had noticed her loss.

So this was what casual scrumping had led to!

Val had thought nothing of pinching a stray apple or cake, and now here he was stealing money.

Going at a brisk walk, but not really running, he slid into one of the back alleys that ran behind the High Street. The purse was burning in his pocket. He was so scared at what he had done that his mouth was dry and his legs felt weak at the knees. At all costs, he must avoid any tangle with the gang or with the police until he had got safe home and hidden the purse.

As soon as he reached the flat, he locked himself in the lavatory so as to examine the purse in peace. With fingers that trembled, he opened the snap of its inner compartment, and found forty pounds and a selection of silver coins. Enough money to buy a second-hand bicycle!

He did not feel particularly guilty now that he was safe at home. The lady at the counter had never seen him, and would not be able to describe him. No one else had noticed him, for there was such a crush around the stall. He had really committed the perfect crime.

But while he stood there looking at the money, he realised that there were still complications. He could not go out and buy a bike, for his parents would at once wonder where he had got the money.

What a fool he was! Why hadn't he thought of that before? He left the lavatory, went into his room, and sat down on the bed. He had been a thief all to no purpose. Then suddenly he saw what he must do. He would have to pretend to get a job. This would mean he would have to disappear every Saturday, and on most evenings. No one in the family would have the time or the energy to check up as to where he went.

For the time being, he shoved the purse under his mattress. But before he did so, he extracted some of the coins, because it would be nice to buy sweets or cigarettes or even go to the pictures after all those weeks without any pocket-money.

He strolled nonchalantly across the yard and marched into the tobacconist, and said, "Dad wants a couple of toofers, please." Toofers were small black cigars which Dad sometimes bought for a treat. When Val got to the Common he started to get his toofer going and then made his way back home. Puffing at his toofer like a steam engine, Val strolled across the yard and up the stairs towards his flat. But as he came to the top flight, he suddenly felt so strange and dizzy that he was forced to sit down on a stair, and the half smoked toofer fell from his fingers on to the concrete floor.

Mum found him there as she went out to do her shopping. He was sitting with his head against the wall, his eyes closed and the toofer lay at his feet.

"Cor, Val, whatever. . . ?"

He opened his eyes and struggled to rise, but his cheeks were green beneath their layer of dirt.

Then Mum saw the toofer, and asked, "Where did you get that thing?"

"Someone gave it me." Even in his last extremity Val could still think.

"Get on!" Mum knew Val well enough to recognize a lie, and with one quick movement she frisked him. There was the jingle of money as she touched his side, and she plunged her hand into his pocket, crying, "Where did you get that from?"

Val's brain, fuddled by the toofer, moved slower than usual, and there was quite a perceptible pause before he answered, "I earned it."

"Come again!" cried Mum. "That won't wash! You'll come right back to the flat with me, my lord. I've got one or two things to ask you!"

In the living-room, Mum faced Val. "Have you been scrumping?"

"No."

"You have, and don't you lie to me." She took a step forward, her usually smiling face drawn and worried. "Where'd you get that money, Val? Give it here. I know Dad and I didn't give you any, so you can't have got it honestly. When I tell your Dad he won't half give you a leathering."

"Mum! Oh, no!" Val put the armchair between himself and Mum, for in spite of her good temper she could be really angry if roused.

"Tell me the truth!" she cried. "And give me that money. Where did you get it?"

Very slowly and unwillingly, Val produced the money coin by coin. He hoped to keep back some, but Mum went on waiting with outstretched hand until he had disgorged all of the remaining silver. When she had got it, Mum went on with her catechism.

"Where did you get it?"

"I – I found it."

"Where?"

Val was feeling too sick to think up a good story, so he came out with the truth. "In the Supermarket."

"How do you mean, found?"

"It was on a stall."

"So, you've been whipping the change?"

"No, no." All the time, Val had been edging nearer and nearer to the door, so as to be ready to make a dash for it, if he could distract Mum's attention for just one second. But she was too quick for him. She dodged round to the door herself and grabbed his wrist.

"Now I'll have the truth out of you, Val Berners, if I have to beat it out. Whose is this money?"

Val began to redden. "Someone dropped their purse."

"That's another lie," said Mum. "Where's the purse then?"

Val saw that he had been silly to mention the purse. "I threw it away," he said.

"And that's another lie," said Mum, who was by now very angry indeed, angry and horrified to find out that her son was a thief. She grabbed hold of Val, crying, "You give me that purse at once."

Val fought and struggled to get away from her, but Mum held on tight. "I won't, I can't," he sobbed, for he could not let go his only chance of a bike.

"Where did you hide it?" Mum shook him hard, and this on top of the toofer finished Val's defiance. "If you don't tell me, I'll go to the police and have you put away."

When at last he confessed it was under his mattress, Mum marched straight to the bed and drew out the purse. The line of her mouth was grim.

"You're a thief, a dirty little sneaking thief!" she cried and slapped him hard across the cheek. "Your Grandpa and Grandma would die of shame if they knew what you'd done. Dad and me's brought you up honest. We never cheated anyone in our lives, and now look at you! Dirty, low cheat!" Mum suddenly collapsed, the anger died out of her and she sank into a chair and began to sob bitterly.

Val stood by, staring at her, horrified. In all his life he had never seen Mum cry before. She had never before slapped his face. Now she had called him a dirty little sneak, thief and a cheat, and all his pride was outraged. He had never thought of himself as a thief. His scrumping had just been an adventure, even his taking of the purse was not stealing, but a revenge on people who would not let him earn money. But Mum had said he was a disgrace, a shame to the family. She called him a thief. He couldn't be that. He wasn't that. But then, what was he?

"How could you do it, Val?" Mum was sobbing. "How could you? I brought you up decent. I've done everything I could to give you clothes and proper food. I got up early and went to work, even when I was ill. And now look what you've done! It's all been no good." And she sobbed more bitterly than ever, feeling the whole defeat, the waste of the bad nights during Val's teething, her savings spent on his first little trousers, his pop gun, his school shoes, his summer holiday. All she had done for him was a sheer loss if he were to grow up a thief.

By this time, the tears were pouring down Val's cheeks, too, making tunnels in the general grime. He turned from his mother to hide his trembling mouth. He couldn't cry in front of any woman, not even his mother.

"I wanted a bike," he said. "All the other boys have got bikes."

"I'd have given you a bike if I'd had the money," sobbed Mum. "You know that, Val, but to steal it – oh!"

"I didn't want to steal for it," said Val. "I tried to get a job, but no one would take me. I asked everywhere." He was walking about the room, banging unseeingly into the chairs and tables. "They laughed at me –

they said – they said . . ." and he was weeping too.

Presently they both got calmer.

"I was so proud of you, Val," said Mum in a sorrowful voice. "You don't know. And so was Dad. We both thought the world of you."

Val had to face the devastating thought that his parents would never be so proud of him again.

Prayer

It is so easy to forget that our actions often affect those who love us. Help us to consider others before we act.

Myth and Folklore

Reading

Talking Brought Me Here, *a Nupe folk tale from Africa.*

A hunter found a human skull in the forest. Surprised, he asked him, "What brought you here?"

The skull answered: "Talking brought me here."

Amazed, the hunter ran home to report to the king, "I have found a skull in the forest who talks!"

The king could not believe it, but he came along with his guard to find out the truth. When they came to the skull, the hunter asked as before, "What brought you here?"

But the skull remained silent.

The angry king called the hunter a liar and ordered the guard to cut off his head and leave it behind as prey for the ants of the forest.

When everyone had left, the skull spoke again, and asked the head of the hunter: "What brought you here?"

And the head gave the answer, "Talking brought me here."

I wonder what you made of that strange little tale? Perhaps it brought to mind a time when you had talked out of turn and caused someone to be angry or upset at what had been said.

So many quarrels seem to start from an "innocent" throw-away remark, which in turn is picked up by someone else and then someone else, until the little remark is blown up out of all proportion. The truth is often distorted as the rumour spreads, and before long great damage can be the result. We call such spreading of tales GOSSIP and let's be honest, haven't we all indulged in it at one time or another?

Can you remember the last time you started a conversation with something like, ". . . Don't say anything, but . . ." or, . . . "John said that Susan said she wasn't going with Dave anymore. . . ."?

What did you do then with the choice bit of gossip? I bet you passed it on in conversation to your mates! It's such a simple trap to tumble into, but such a difficult one to get out of once a story has circulated. Perhaps the little fable we heard at the start might make us aware that gossip and the spreading of rumours can lead to all sorts of problems – maybe not quite so drastic as the conclusion of the folk tale – but nevertheless we should be careful about our use of words. If a friend confides in us, then we should respect that confidence. There is nothing that can destroy a friendship so rapidly as a lack of trust. Hearing something you told in confidence to your friend being discussed by all manner of other people is a sure sign that your trust has been broken. That's when the anger and the hurt break through. That's when the quarrels start. That's when "Talking brought me here . . ."

Prayer

Help me to know when to keep silent and when to speak out.

Futures

Reading

Snakes and Ladders by *Frances Pinnock (aged 15)*

My life is a game of snakes and ladders,
There is no set pattern: every move I make
Has a result, a beginning, an end,
And is scrutinized by those ready to pounce,
To condemn, to ridicule, to tear to pieces.
Every day is spent running up ladders of nonentity
And crashing down snakes of reality,
Like black stone power-stations, or a forgotten
Thanatoid building of desolation, blocking, spoiling,
Deliberately concealing any pleasing view behind them,
The view of which I crave for,
Like an addict craves his drugs.

Sometimes I come to a ladder:
A visit to russet Hyde Park in October,
Praise from my teacher,
A new Presley record,
An excursion to the theatre –
Selfish things, but what a joy they bring to me
In those precious moments before I am hurtled back to
                                                    reality.
Dear God, will I ever be allowed to pass into womanhood,
Into an existence of responsibility,
Of happy living, of a husband and children?
Or will I be struck down,
Blinded by that unquenchable horrifying threat
That hangs over the world like a heavy, black,
Blanket of destruction?

Are you going to allow me to know, to feel,
To experience cold, hard-living death by radioactivity?
Am I ever going to bring up children
Without fear of mocking them?
To bring them into this red-hot world
Sitting on an active volcano?
Inside me there are endless voices
Cawing in triumph like crows, black and ugly,
Crying, "Destruction! Death! Uselessness!"
And asking one question – the vital question:
Will I ever be allowed to grow up?

Someone once said that "adolescence is a time of stress and storms"
meaning that many anxieties and worries crowd into already busy
young lives. Many of you here today will have had some sort of
argument with your parents or guardians over such issues as:

the kinds of friends you go around with – "I don't like you mixing
with that crowd . . ."

the time you come in at night – "What time do you call this?"

the clothes you wear – "You're not going out looking like that . . ."

the way you speak to people – "Don't talk to me in that tone of
voice . . ."

the time when you want to be on your own – "And don't you go off in
a sulk again . . ."

The list seems endless and it's all because you are taking that
enormous stride from the world of childhood to the world of the adult
and it's a frightening prospect. There are times when you want to cling
to the security of childhood and yet yearn to be treated like an adult.
One of the biggest steps is when you leave school and this poem was
written by someone who looked back at her school days very positively:

The Rusty Blue Gateway by *Helen Howard (aged 16)*

As the rusty blue gateway became just a memory,
And the people she'd known, a handful of security.
The 'would-be' schoolgirl opened up a different world.
The gates that had held her, and the friends that had laughed,
Were past. . . .

Today was proof it didn't last.
Her battle line against the world,
A new adjustment never found.
She faced the sky . . .
The clouds above began to cry,
The chalky walls that held her pain,
Were holding out the driving rain.
The schoolgirl turned and looked again,
With new eyes, she closed behind her the rusty blue gateway.
A final smile,
Tomorrow's woman, with thanks to yesterday's people.

Prayer

Whatever the future holds for us, may we face it with courage and hope.

Honesty

Reading

Crime Never Pays by *David Maton (aged 15)*

When we are young there are so many lessons to learn. Some we learn very easily but others seem to take a long time to 'sink in'. In the reading that follows we hear how a little child came to realize for himself that 'Crime Never Pays'.

Temptation comes in many forms, but it can often stem from the fact that someone has something we do not and we feel the immediate, desperate need for that thing – whatever it is. So, rather than reason sensibly and think about the ways we could legitimately obtain the item, we are tempted – we choose to 'take the easy way'. It is something, I am sure, we have all done at some stage in our lives. The problem is when the 'easy way' becomes a habit, an accepted way of life and the pang of conscience is no longer felt. When we are young, very often our 'conscience' looms in the guise of a parent or guardian (as in the following story) but when we are older *we alone* make the choices. It is hard sometimes, when all our friends take that easy road, for us to stride alone along the right track, guided by our conscience; but remember those simple, early lessons. It is far less complicated living with a clear conscience than one shackled by all sorts of dark secrets. To be a successful liar one needs a fantastic memory and surely life is much happier without having to think up a devious story before speaking? Still, some people choose that path. . . .

> "Crime Never Pays"
> Whenenever I hear this phrase
> I think back to my early days.
> I could have been no more than four,
> When I toddled to our local store
> With my Mother, to get some bread,
> "And other necessities," she said.
> It was the shop just off my street,

And it sold every kind of sweet.
Well, being just so very little,
Sherberts, allsorts and peanut brittle
Seemed so tempting to a child,
So, I turned to Mum and sweetly smiled.
I asked her so nicely for some sweets,
Pear drops, liquorice, a little treat?
My Mother said, "No way, young man,"
And continued looking for the ham.
"You're going to see the dentist!"
"Well," I thought, "I can't cope with this."
So, accidentally, you understand,
I reached out my little hand
And, with a sidelong glance at Mum
Pocketed a pack of chewing gum.

Sitting in our car, on the back seat,
I opened up my little treat.
When at the dentist's we arrived
To hide the gum I then contrived,
And, being just so very young
I hid it just beneath my tongue.
When the dentist said, "Say Ah,"
I looked across the room at Ma.

Well, when he told Mum what he'd found,
My feet, they never touched the ground.
She took me home and to my gloom
Ordered me upstairs to my room.
This story is, in fact, quite true,
I hope from my mistakes that you
Have learnt that crime will never pay,
And honesty will win the day.

Prayer

May we remember this simple story when we are tempted
to "take the easy way".

Loss of Freedom

Reading

Taken to a Cell by *Arthur Koestler*, from **Dialogue With Death**

Then I was taken to a cell.

For the first time I heard the sound of a cell door being slammed from the outside.

It is a unique sound. A cell door has no handle, either outside or inside; it cannot be shut except by being slammed to. It is made of massive steel and concrete, about four inches thick, and every time it falls to there is a resounding crash just as though a shot has been fired. But this report dies away without an echo. Prison sounds are echo-less and bleak.

When the door has been slammed behind him for the first time, the prisoner stands in the middle of the cell and looks around. I fancy that everyone must behave in more or less the same way.

First of all he gives a fleeting look round the walls and takes a mental inventory of all the objects in what is now his domain:
the iron bedstead,
the wash-basin,
the W.C.,
the barred window.

His next act is invariably to try to pull himself up by the iron bars of the window and look out. He fails, and his suit is covered with white from the plaster on the wall against which he has pressed himself.

He desists, but decides to practise and master the art of pulling himself up by his hands. Indeed, he makes all sorts of laudable resolutions; he will do exercises every morning and learn a foreign language, and he simply won't let his spirit be broken. He dusts his suit and continues his voyage of exploration round his puny realm – five paces long by four paces broad. He tries the iron bedstead. The springs are broken, the wire mattress sags and cuts into the flesh; it's like lying in a hammock made of steel wire. He pulls a face, being determined to prove that he is full of courage and confidence. Then his gaze rests on the cell door, and sees that an eye is glued to the spy-hole and is watching him.

The eye goggles at him glassily, its pupil unbelievably big; it is an eye without a man attached to it, and for a few moments the prisoner's heart stops beating.

The eye disappears and the prisoner takes a deep breath and presses his hand against the left side of his chest.

"Now, then," he says to himself encouragingly, "how silly to go and get so frightened. You must get used to that; after all, the official's only doing his duty by peeping in; that's part of being in prison. But they won't get me down; I'll stuff paper in the spy-hole at night. . . ."

As a matter of fact there's no reason why he shouldn't do so straight away. The idea fills him with genuine enthusiasm. For the first time he experiences that almost manic desire for activity that from now on will alternate continually – up and down in a never-ending zig-zag – with melancholia and depression.

Then he realises that he has no paper on him, and his next impulse is – according to his social status – either to ring or to run over to the stationer's at the corner. This impulse lasts only the fraction of a second; the next moment he becomes conscious for the first time of the true significance of his situation. For the first time he grasps the full reality of being behind a door which is locked from outside, grasps it in all its searing, devastating poignancy.

This, too, lasts only a few seconds. The next moment the anaesthetizing mechanism gets going again, and brings about that merciful state of semi-narcosis induced by pacing up and down, forging plans, weaving illusions.

"Let's see," says the novice, "where were we? Ah, yes, that business of stuffing paper in the spy-hole. It *must* be possible to get hold of paper somehow or other." He leaves the "how" in this "somehow" suspended in mid-air. This is a mode of thought that he will soon master – or, rather it will master him. "When I get out," he will say for example, "I shall never worry about money again. I shall run along somehow or other." Or: "When I get out, I shall never quarrel with the wife again. We'll manage to get along somehow."

Indeed, "somehow or other" everything will be all right once he's free.

The fact that the prisoner follows this stereotyped line of thought, which, as I say, is going, after a few days, to master him, means that the outside world increasingly loses its reality for him; it becomes a dream world in which everything is somehow or other possible.

"Where were we? . . . Oh, yes, that business of stuffing paper in the spy-hole. Of course, somehow or other one can get hold of some paper. But is it allowed? No, it's certain not to be allowed. So why bother?

"Let's take a more thorough inventory of the objects in the room. Why, look, there's an iron table with a chair which we haven't observed or fully appreciated yet. Of course the chair can't be moved from the table; it's welded to it. A pity, otherwise one might use it as a bed table and put one's things on it when getting undressed – pocket-book, handkerchief, cigarettes, matches and so on. . . ."

Then it occurs to him that he has neither pocket-book nor handkerchief, cigarettes nor matches in his pocket.

The barometer of his mood falls a second time.

It rises again the moment he has tried the tap over the wash-basin. "Look, there's running water in prison – it isn't half as bad as one imagined from outside. After all, there is a bed (and it's much healthier to sleep on a hard bed), a wash-basin, a table, a chair – what more does a man need? One must learn to live simply and unassumingly: a few exercises, reading, writing, learning a foreign language. . . ."

The next voyage of discovery is in the direction of the water closet. "Why there's even one of these – it's really not half so bad." He pulls the plug. The chain refuses to function. And the barometer falls afresh.

It rises again once the subtle plan has been conceived of filling the bucket with water from the tap and flushing the lavatory pan in this way. It falls again when it transpires that the tap has also ceased to function. It rises again when he reflects that there must be certain times of the day when the water runs. It falls – it rises – it falls – it rises. And this is how things are going to go on – in the coming minutes, hours, days, weeks, years.

How long has he already been in the cell?

He looks at this watch: exactly three minutes.

Prayer

We accept freedom so carelessly. It is only when it is taken away from us that we realize what a responsibility it is. For a moment, let us think of those who have lost their freedom and also how *we* use our freedom.

Talents

Use what talents you possess;
The woods would be very silent if
No birds sang there except
Those that sang best.
by Van Dykes

Reading

My School Days by *Lenny Henry*

I was always late for school because when your dad goes out at 5am and your mum works as well, she leaves these chores for you to do. Consequently I had this Mission Impossible to achieve, with a list of things like going to the shops to buy vegetables, and by the time I finished it was probably five to nine. You got the stick, which was about three feet long and an inch thick, if you were late, even if you explained. I know there are some who say there is no substitute for a good clout around the ear, but I used to think it was so cruel. It would bring tears to your eyes, but you couldn't cry because all your friends would be there watching.

I went to St James's Infants' School, Dudley, in the West Midlands, and I loved it. I loved the play, the kind of stuff they did with sand and water. Then came the shock of primary school – I went to Jesson's Junior School – when things got harder and you had to learn about geography and stuff. It got very heavy. When we moved house, a couple of miles away, I had to go to another junior school, St John's, and everything changed. I think we were all a bit naive at Jesson's. There were more black and Asian kids at St John's and it was tougher. I heard my first swear words in the playground and was quite shocked by it all.

I remember on my first day I had these new gloves and I lost them. We all searched but couldn't find them. I was really upset. Then I looked in my pocket and they were there. I never told anybody, so I had these gloves that were really nice and warm but I didn't dare wear them.

I didn't go to grammar school because I failed the second half of the 11-plus. Academically I wasn't that forceful, so I went to Bluecoat Secondary Modern, another Church of England school.

We had a special uniform. It was quite posh. We were streamed into classes that sounded like experimental rockets. The top stream was 3X1 and the stream below that was 3X2. I was in 3X2. You kind of felt it was inferior because you knew 3X1 were going to take O levels and you were just going to do CSE's. I don't know what my school reports were like. I didn't read them. My mum read them and I just remember being locked in my bedroom for a long time.

I was really bad at sports. I didn't like running, didn't like the cold, didn't like other people depending on me to get the baton or score the goal or whatever. But if there was any fun to be had, mimicking or tomfoolery, I wanted to be involved in that. I never got the cane, but I was the kind of kid who got caught. I had a sign over my head saying, 'It was him'. I had one of those faces and I was always giggling, which gave the game away. I played truant once or twice, but it was dreadful. Truant is about going out and having a really great time, but you always went down town, walked around the shops, and everybody saw you. Teachers would nip out and get some fags or something and they'd catch you there.

I wasn't a prefect but my sister was and I was jealous of her. She was very good and they used to say to me all the time "your sister this" and "your sister that". It just made you think, "Oh well, she's done it all, what's left for me to do?"

There is something in me that didn't want to have anything to do with violence and I never got involved in any fights, although I remember when I was older a new boy from Jamaica trying to pick a fight. I thought it was stupid.

One teacher I gravitated towards because he had a good sense of humour was our science master. He encouraged me to set up a radio with a little speaker and a microphone in the back room, and we'd make silly tapes, pretending to be the Goon Show. He was a hip teacher.

I never really sussed out the education system. At school there were too many other distractions – girls, clothes. The whole socio-political arena around you was changing, so consequently you had more important things on your mind than whether you were going to make that maths test. Unless you were a particular type of person, a stoic or completely blinkered, that is the only way to go through school. Or if you go to one where every day it is hammered into you. At our school it wasn't like that. If you learnt, you learnt; if you didn't you didn't.

I did my O levels when I was in Blackpool for 23 weeks in 1984. I was so surprised because I always had this feeling that I am a bit thick or a bit slow, but I'm not. The need to learn something is what makes you understand. If you really want to do it, you'll do it. I only wish I'd known that then.

> **Prayer**
>
> Sometimes we may wonder what our lives hold in store for us. May we always give of our best in whatever we do.

Thank You

Reading

Thank You M'am by *Langston Hughes*

She was a large woman with a large purse that had everything in it but a hammer and nails. It had a long strap, and she carried it slung across her shoulder. It was about eleven o'clock at night, dark, and she was walking alone, when a boy ran up behind her and tried to snatch her purse. The strap broke with the sudden single tug the boy gave it from behind. But the boy's weight and the weight of the purse combined to cause him to lose his balance. Instead of taking off full blast as he had hoped, the boy fell on his back on the sidewalk and his legs flew up. The large woman simply turned around and kicked him right square in his blue-jeaned sitter. Then she reached down, picked the boy up by his shirt front, and shook him until his teeth rattled.

After that the woman said, "Pick up my pocket-book, boy, and give it here."

She still held him tightly. But she bent down enough to permit him to stoop and pick up her purse. Then she said, "Now ain't you ashamed of yourself?"

Firmly gripped by his shirt front, the boy said, "Yes'm."

The woman said, "What did you want to do it for?"

The boy said, "I didn't aim to."

She said, "You tell a lie!"

By that time two or three people passed, stopped, turned to look, and some stood watching.

"If I turn you loose, will you run?" asked the woman.

"Yes'm," said the boy.

"Then I won't turn you loose," said the woman. She did not release him.

"Lady, I'm sorry," whispered the boy.

"Um-hum! Your face is dirty. I got a great mind to wash your face for you. Ain't you got nobody home to tell you to wash your face?"

"No'm," said the boy.

"Then it will get washed this evening," said the large woman, starting up the street, dragging the frightened boy behind her.

He looked as if he were fourteen or fifteen, frail and willow-wild, in tennis shoes and blue jeans.

The woman said, "You ought to be my son. I would teach you right from wrong. Least I can do right now is to wash your face. Are you hungry?"

"No'm," said the being-dragged boy. "I just want you to turn me loose."

"Was I bothering *you* when I turned that corner?" the woman asked.

"No'm."

"But you put yourself in contact with *me*," said the woman. "If you think that that contact is not going to last awhile, you got another thought coming. When I get through with you, sir, you are going to remember Mrs Luella Bates Washington Jones."

Sweat popped out onto the boy's face and he began to struggle. Mrs Jones stopped, jerked him around in front of her, put a half-nelson about his neck, and continued to drag him up the street. When she got to her door, she dragged the boy inside, down a hall, and into a large kitchenette-furnished room at the rear of the house. She switched on the light and left the door open. The boy could hear other roomers laughing and talking in the large house. Some of their doors were open, too, so he knew he and the woman were not alone. The woman still had him by the neck in the middle of her room.

She said, "What is your name?"

"Roger," answered the boy.

"Then, Roger, you go to that sink and wash your face," said the woman, whereupon she turned him loose – at last. Roger looked at the door – looked at the woman – *and went to the sink.*

"Let the water run until it gets warm," she said. "Here's a clean towel."

"You gonna take me to jail?" asked the boy, bending over the sink.

"Not with that face, I would not take you nowhere," said the woman. "Here I am trying to get home to cook me a bite to eat, and you snatch my pocketbook! Maybe you ain't been to your supper either, late as it be. Have you?"

"There's nobody home at my house," said the boy.

"Then we'll eat," said the woman. I believe you're hungry – or been hungry – to try to snatch my pocketbook!"

"I want a pair of blue suede shoes," said the boy.

"Well, you didn't have to snatch *my* pocketbook to get some suede shoes," said Mrs Luella Bates Washington Jones. "You could of asked me."

"M'am?"

The water dripping from his face, the boy looked at her. There was a long pause. A very long pause. After he had dried his face, and not knowing what else to do, dried it again, the boy turned around, wondering what next. The door was open. He could make a dash for it down the hall. He could run, run, run, *run*!

The woman was sitting on the daybed. After a while she said, "I were young once and I wanted things I could not get."

There was another long pause. The boy's mouth opened. Then he frowned, not knowing he frowned.

The woman said, "Um-hum! You thought I was going to say but, didn't you? You thought I was going to say, *but I didn't snatch people's pocketbooks*. Well, I wasn't going to say that." Pause. Silence. "I have done things too, which I would not tell you, son – neither tell God if He didn't already know. Everybody's got something in common. So you sit down while I fix us something to eat. You might run that comb through your hair so you will look presentable."

In another corner of the room behind a screen was a gas plate and an icebox. Mrs Jones got up and went behind the screen. The woman did not watch the boy to see if he was going to run now, nor did she watch her purse, which she left behind her on the daybed. But the boy took care to sit on the far side of the room, away from the purse, where he thought she could easily see him out of the corner of her eye if she wanted to. He did not trust the woman *not* to trust him. And he did not want to be mistrusted now.

"Do you need somebody to go to the store," asked the boy, "maybe to get some milk or something?"

"Don't believe I do," said the woman, "unless you just want sweet milk yourself. I was going to make cocoa out of this canned milk I got here."

"That will be fine," said the boy.

She heated some lima beans and ham she had in the icebox, made the cocoa, and set the table. The woman did not ask the boy anything about where he lived, or his folks, or anything else that would embarrass him. Instead, as they ate, she told him about her job in a hotel beauty shop that stayed open late, what work was like, and how all kinds of women came in and out, blondes, redheads, and Spanish. Then she cut him half of her ten cent cake.

"Eat some more, son," she said.

When they were finished eating, she got up and said, "Now here take this ten dollars and buy yourself some blue suede shoes. And next time, do not make the mistake of latching onto *my* pocketbook *nor anybody else's* because shoes got by devilish ways will burn your feet. I got to get my rest now. But from here on, son, I hope you will behave yourself."

She led him down the hall to the front door and opened it. "Good night! Behave yourself, boy!" she said looking out into the street as he went down the steps.

The boy wanted to say something other than "Thank you, m'am," to Mrs Luella Bates Washington Jones, but although his lips moved, he couldn't even say that as he turned at the foot of the barren step and looked at the large woman in the door. Then she shut the door.

Prayer

Sometimes our lives are influenced by the most unlikely people and events. May we be aware when those moments happen.

Author index

Index of titles of readings

Index of suggested themes

The following are *suggestions* only, as many of the readings can be adapted to fit a number of different themes as interpreted by the reader